HEY MOM, I'M BORED!

D1274246

HEY MOM, I'M BORED!

100

games,

activities, and

brain teasers

to keep kids of all ages entertained

From the authors of *TravelMates*

Story Evans and Lise O'Haire

145375

THREE RIVERS PRESS
NEW YORK

Published by Three Rivers Press, New York, New York.
Member of the Crown Publishing Group.

Random House, Inc. New York, Toronto, London, Sydney, Auckland
www.randomhouse.com

Three Rivers Press is a registered trademark and the Three Rivers
Press colophon is a trademark of Random House, Inc.

Printed in the United States of America

Designed by Karen Minster

Library of Congress Cataloging-in-Publication Data
Evans, Story.
   Hey mom, I'm bored! : 100 games, activities, and brain teasers to
keep kids of all ages entertained / by Story Evans and Lise O'Haire.
     p. cm.
   Includes index.
   1. Games.   I. Title: 100 games, activities, and brain teasers to
keep kids of all ages entertained.   II. O'Haire, Lise.   III. Title.
GV1203.E83 2000   790.1'922—dc21   99-59996

ISBN 0-609-80447-2

10 9 8 7 6 5 4 3 2 1

First Edition

THIS BOOK IS DEDICATED TO

Our parents, who always encourage us: Judy and Carl Shem, Connie Nussbaum, and in loving memory of John Nussbaum.

Our children, Abby, Chelsea, Drew, Madeleine, Maggie, Mandi, McCrea, Megan, and cousin Fee Shem, who inspire our laughter and creativity.

Tony and Michael, our husbands, who love whatever we do.

Our siblings, who were the first to play with us: Casey, Bill, Penny, Diane, Suzanne, John, and Rob.

Ann Jacob's 1998–99 third-grade class at Morris Brandon Elementary School and Loretta Fine and Eileen Godwin's 1998–99 third-grade class at Trinity School, with grateful appreciation.

Janet Spencer King, our friend and agent.

All of our friends and our children's friends, who were actively involved in the process and encouraged us all the way.

And special thanks to Brian Balocki, Susan Bryant, Katie Patterson, Barbara Robertson, Ann Stevens, Mats Vlahantonis, Patty Weeks, and Joan Wyman.

AUTHORS' NOTE

This collection of back-to-basics classic children's games was developed from numerous sources. Many of these games have been passed from generation to generation. Others have been invented or reinvented by the authors, their children, and friends.

CONTENTS

INTRODUCTION

Boredom blues . . . how often have you heard *your* child say, "Hey Mom, I'm bored! There's nothing to do."

Rain or shine, inside or out, on vacation or at home, this book will entertain the blues away. There are games for all ages, from preschoolers on up, even some Mom and Dad will enjoy, games that keep all ages happily occupied for many hours.

For many generations, kids entertained themselves—and each other—with time-tested games that challenged their bodies and minds. Today's children, though, turn to the TV, to video games, and to the computer to fill the hours. But electronic wizardry, for all its allure, can't take the place of spontaneous, inventive, active play—the kind children discover when they play classic games.

For this book, the authors of *TravelMates* researched outdoor, backyard, and recess games, many of which have been around for decades, if not centuries. They've updated them when necessary and added a creative twist of their own here and there; *plus, there are brand-new games as well.* None of these games requires hard-to-find supplies; most of them don't need anything beyond what you probably already have in your kitchen drawers.

So join in the fun! Enough with the boredom—let the games begin.

HELPFUL HINTS FOR PLAYING

Game Descriptions

For quick reference we thought it would be useful for players to have a snapshot of each game. At the top of each game outline you will find a summary including the following:

Number of players or teams

Location (indoors or outdoors)

Equipment

Energy level

    Calm: low-key, quiet, mellow, relaxed

    Lively: increased action level, spirited

    Action-packed: high gear, enthusiastic, rambunctious, lots of movement

Type of game

Arts/Imagination	Clapping	Hunting	Racing	Tagging
Backward	Copying	Jumping	Relay	Tapping
Balancing	Dodging	Laughing	Rolling	Throwing/Catching
Blindfold/Guessing	Guessing	Memory	Running	Tossing
Bouncing/Volley	Hide-and-Seek	Obstacle	Strategy	Tugging

Game Guidelines

HOW TO CHOOSE PLAYERS OR TEAMS   There are a variety of ways to choose players and teams or who goes first.

Number all players: Even numbers create one team, odd numbers create the other team; low numbers start first.

Alphabet letters: Assign letters beginning with A and proceeding in alphabetical order. A, C, E, and so on are one team and B, D, F, and so on are the other team; the last letter given out goes first.

Draw from a deck of cards: This works best for choosing which player goes first; high card or low card—player's choice.

Hair or eye color: Put players in teams based on hair or eye color.

Coin toss: Players toss coin. Heads form one team, tails the other team; heads goes first, tails goes second.

Birthdays: January to June is one team, July to December the other team; the youngest player goes first.

If the method creates uneven teams, assign the youngest child to the larger team.

HOW TO HANDLE HURT FEELINGS   No one likes it when the game does not go his or her way. How do you handle the hurt feelings that can result? Many times the best approach is to start fresh, move on completely (past the stumbling block of disappointment), and choose another game.

Playing is fun and that is what games are all about. Playing with friends and being good sports are some of life's simple pleasures.

FUN FOR ALL AGES   The games in this section are included here because they spanned more than one of our age groups, but not all of the games are appropriate for everyone. If you are a parent with a four or five-year-old, make sure you read the description all the way through before involving your child.

PRE-K AND KINDERGARTEN:
Ready to Play

Duck, Duck, Goose

Number of players: 6 or more
Location: Outdoors
Equipment: None

Energy level: Lively
Type of game: Tagging

Duck, duck, who's the goose? To start this classic game, all the players sit in a circle and one is chosen to be the goose, or It. The other players are ducks. The object of the game is for It to find a new goose.

The goose walks around the outside of the circle saying the word "duck," as she gently taps each player's head. At some point she will say "goose" instead of duck. That player immediately jumps up and chases It around the circle. If the tapped player cannot tag It before It sits down in the open space the player left, then he becomes the new goose. If he does tag It, then It continues as the goose.

The new goose moves around the circle repeating "duck, duck, duck, duck" until he decides on a goose!

For a twist, have the players stand in a circle holding hands. In this version, the goose taps shoulders saying "duck, duck, duck." Once a player is tapped with the word goose, she drops the hands she was holding, and chases the goose around the circle, while the other players reconnect. The goose must remember the exact spot where he tapped the player and then scoot underneath the hands into the center of the circle. If the goose cannot make it into the circle, or is tagged, then the goose is still It.

Roly Poly

Number of players: 1 or more
Location: Outdoors
Equipment: None
Energy level: Lively
Type of game: Rolling

Roly Poly rolled away. Roly Poly had a great day. No winners, no losers, just frolicking fun. The object of this game is to roll as far and as fast as you can. Lie down on the ground; on the count of three, start rolling. How fast can you go? How far can you go? Can you roll singing a song?

For a twist, 2 players lie down on their stomachs stretching their arms toward each other, holding hands. Start rolling together. If enough players, have a team race. Roll along, Roly Poly.

Thumbs Up 7-Up

Number of players: 9 or more
Location: Indoors or Outdoors
Equipment: None

Energy level: Lively
Type of game: Guessing

This is a good guessing game for a gathering of friends. Depending on the size of the group, choose 2 (for a group of about 9) to 4 (for a group of 10 or more) players to be the thumb pushers. The object of this game is to identify who pushed your thumb down while your eyes were shut.

The thumb pushers stand in front of the group while the rest of the group close their eyes and cover them with the crook of one elbow. If inside, play at a table and rest your head nestled in one arm on the table. If you're outside, sit down with your knees up, your arm resting on your knees, and your head nestled in your arm. Make your free hand into a fist, keeping the thumb up.

After everyone is in position, the thumb pushers call out, "Thumbs Up 7-Up." In silence the thumb pushers move around the group pushing players' thumbs down at random. Not all thumbs will be pushed down. When done, the thumb pushers walk to the front of the group and call out, "Stand Up 7-Up," and all players whose thumbs were pushed down stand.

You have only one guess to identify who pushed your thumb down. Guessing correctly allows you to be a thumb pusher in the next round. If no one guesses correctly, start another round with the same thumb pushers.

Thumbs up, thumbs down, who's to know?

Nature's Creations

Number of players: 1 or more
Location: Outdoors
Equipment: None

Energy level: Calm
Type of game: Arts/Imagination

Imagine that the beach, yard, woods, or park is a blank canvas and you are the artist. The object of this game is to collect 10 items, such as shells, seaweed, twigs, sand, moss, leaves, small stones, pinecones, flower petals, and grass. Find a flat place, lay out the goodies, and use them to create a design, sculpture, or picture.

If there are many players, divide into 2 groups. As a group, collect 20 or more of nature's creations. Create away. Which group has the most colorful, silly, or beautiful piece of art?

Food, Glorious Food

Number of players: 2 or more
Location: Indoors
Equipment: None

Energy level: Calm
Type of game: Arts/Imagination

A strawberry is a strawberry is a strawberry, but what else could it be? Strawberry jelly, strawberry milkshake, strawberry sherbet, strawberry shortcake. The object of this game is to name a food, repeat it three times, and then think of what other kinds of food it could be.

To play this game one player decides on a food such as chocolate, and says, "Chocolate is chocolate is chocolate, but what else could it be?" The other players respond in turn by saying things like chocolate chip cookie, chocolate ice cream, chocolate cake, chocolate pudding. Players in turn continue with the pattern of choosing a food; repeating it three times, and asking but what else could it be? until everyone runs out of ideas.

Finger Quest

Number of players: 2 or more
Location: Indoors or Outdoors
Equipment: None

Energy level: Calm
Type of game: Guessing

Will you show the same number of fingers as I do? That's the quest. Each player holds her left hand palm up and makes a fist with her right hand. To begin, each player taps her closed fist on her left hand three times and then opens it up showing any number of fingers. The object is to see how often players can match one another.

One, two, three, who knows?

Pirate's Gold

Number of teams: 2 teams of at least 5
Location: Outdoors
Equipment: A coin or small object

Energy level: Action-packed
Type of game: Running

Ahoy, mates, come capture the gold! This game is great for a group. Divide into 2 teams, pirates and navy. Pirates have the gold. Use a small coin, stone, or paper clip to be the gold piece. The object of this game is for the navy team to seize the gold before the pirate who has the gold can get to the navy's side.

To begin, set up the playing field: your backyard, the driveway, the beach, or any area that gives you enough room to be chased. Determine the end zones. Each team meets at its base (the end zone), and the pirates decide who will carry the gold. That player hides it in his fist. Every pirate plays the game with a closed fist so that it is not obvious who has the gold.

Each team lines up in a straight line at its base. At the count of three, the teams run toward each other. The navy team tries to tag any pirate, hoping to capture the gold. When a pirate is tagged, he must freeze and open his fist. If that pirate does not have the gold, the navy team continues to tag members of the pirate team in hopes of getting the gold.

If the tagged pirate does have the gold, the navy player shouts, "Ahoy, mates, we have the gold!" and that round is over. For the next round the teams switch, the navy team becoming the pirate team and the pirate team becoming the navy team. If the pirate who has the gold makes it to the navy end zone without being tagged, the pirate team keeps the gold.

A new round begins with a different pirate holding the gold.

I Spy Pantomime

Number of players: 4 or more
Location: Outdoors
Equipment: None

Energy level: Lively
Type of game: Guessing

A pantomime version of the classic I Spy game. This is best played with a group. The object of this game is to guess correctly what the player in the center of the circle is pantomiming.

Everyone sits in a circle. Choose one player to be the detective. The detective stands in the center of the circle and says, "I spy with my little eyes . . . ," and proceeds to act out what he spies. No limits to what can be spied: a bird flying, driving a car, licking an ice cream cone, sitting in a chair, walking a dog, or the postman delivering mail.

The player who guesses correctly is the next detective. If no one can identify what is being pantomimed after 5 minutes, the player in the center chooses another player to spy something and act it out.

Parading Pennies

Number of players: 1 or more
Location: Indoors or Outdoors
Equipment: 5 pennies for each player

Energy level: Calm
Type of game: Balancing

Can you parade pennies perfectly on your fingers? To start, find 5 pennies for each player. Choose a hand to use. The objective of this game is to move around while balancing pennies on the tips of the fingers on one hand.

Palm up, place a penny on each fingertip. See if you can walk without dropping any. Feeling confident? Try hopping.

Now that you are the penny master, try this. The object is to transfer the pennies from one hand to the other. Slowly touch the unused hand, palm face up, to the hand with the pennies, matching fingertip to fingertip. Now flip both hands over and remove the penniless hand. If you drop any, try again.

What other movements can you do while balancing pennies? Our favorite is standing on one foot and pivoting round and round.

Follow the Leader

Number of players: 3 or more
Location: Indoors or Outdoors
Equipment: None

Energy level: Lively
Type of game: Copying

Are you ready? Okay, let's follow the leader! This classic game can be played inside, walking from room to room, or outside across the yard. The object of this game is to move in a line copying the actions of the leader. Players line up and the player at the front is the first leader. All other players must copy the leader's actions.

If outside, for example, the leader may decide to walk, skip, or run while clapping hands overhead, or snapping fingers, or making up any fun movement to be copied by all. After a minute or two, the leader goes to the end of the line and it's the next player's turn.

To make the game more engaging, add a song or a rhyme to the action.

Lively Letters

Number of players: 2 or more
Location: Indoors or Outdoors
Equipment: None

Energy level: Lively
Type of game: Arts/Imagination

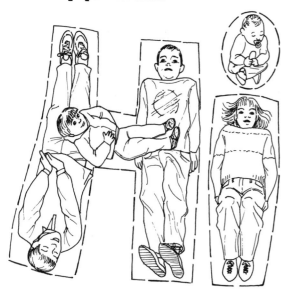

Are you bored writing letters on paper? The object of this game is to make letters using your body. Use your arms, hands, fingers, knees, and legs. Try this: If you bend your right arm, it looks like a *V* going from the top of your shoulder down to your elbow and up to your wrist. What other letters can you make?

Can your friends guess what letter you have just created? Be imaginative. Everyone likes lively letters looking loony!

Red Light, Green Light

Number of players: 5 or more
Location: Outdoors
Equipment: None

Energy level: Lively
Type of game: Running

Red light, green light, you're the stoplight. Let's play. A tried-and-true classic school-yard game. The object of this game is to move from the baseline and to be the first to tag the person who is It.

Choose one player to be It, called the traffic light. All other players move back a good distance, about 100 steps, and line up in a row on what will be known as the baseline.

The player who has been selected as It turns her back to the line and says, "Green light." At this time all players are allowed to move forward. Everyone has to stop when the traffic light calls out, "Red light" and turns to face the group. Anyone who has not stopped moving and is seen by the traffic light is sent back to the baseline to start over. The first player to tag It without being caught is the next traffic light.

Musical Chairs

Number of players: 5 or more
Location: Indoors or Outdoors
Equipment: Music and things to sit on for
  each player minus one

Energy level: Lively
Type of game: Racing

A favorite classic played for generations. The object of this game is to have a spot to sit down when the music stops. All you need is music and something to sit on such as a chair, towel, or pillow. Always use one less seat than the number of players in your group, so there is one player who will not be able to find a seat.

Choose one player to be the musical director who starts and stops the music. When the music starts, the players walk around whatever you have chosen to sit on. The excitement of the game is to find a place to sit down when the music stops. A player will be out when she is left standing, having no seat. Continue in rounds. The winner captures the last seat.

Wiggle, Wobble

Number of players: 5 or more
Location: Outdoors
Equipment: None

Energy level: Lively
Type of game: Rolling

Wiggle, wobble, jiggle, and jive! This game will surely bring out the smiles. All players sit on the ground in a line, legs crossed, shoulder to shoulder. It works best when the line is shaped like the letter S. The player at one end of the line begins the movement by leaning toward the next player, who leans against the next player, and so on. When the movement gets to the last player, he sends it back.

Simple rules: Just let your body flow. Move this way or that way depending on the way the line is turning or moving. Wiggle, wobble and enjoy the motion.

The Beat Goes On

Number of players: 4 or more
Location: Indoors or Outdoors
Equipment: None

Energy level: Lively
Type of game: Copying

We're moving, we're grooving, we're making a beat. The object of this game is to remember the movements created by each player and add a new one.

The first player starts with any movement, such as clapping hands, snapping fingers, or tapping feet. The next player copies the first player's movement and adds a new one. Play continues with each player repeating all the movements in the order they were created and adding a new move to the end of the sequence. If you cannot remember a movement, you are out of the game, but you will be entertained watching the chain of motion. Keep it going as long as you can. The beat goes on.

Amusing ABC's

Number of players: 2 or more
Location: Indoors or Outdoors
Equipment: None

Energy level: Lively
Type of game: Laughing

Most of us know the ABC song. Can you dance while singing your ABC's? Can you hop, do jumping jacks, skip, or clap your hands? The object of this game is to move around while singing the alphabet. Let the song and silliness begin.

Another way to spice up the alphabet is to say it three times, as fast as you can, without laughing or stopping. Then try it in rounds with one player saying A, the next B, and so on until you finish. Now do the same thing, but faster.

Or try singing the alphabet as fast as you can. See who finishes first.

FIRST AND SECOND GRADE:
Watch Me Now

Fortune Teller

Number of players: 2 or more
Location: Indoors or Outdoors
Equipment: None

Energy level: Calm
Type of game: Arts/Imagination

Come one, come all, gather around the fortune teller. The face tells it all. The object of this game is predict your fortune using your face and birth date to find out if you are smart, good-looking, nosy, or a good kisser.

If your birth date is the 11th, for example, begin by counting, 1 for the forehead, 2 for the eyes, 3 for the nose, 4 for the lips, and then repeat forehead, eyes, nose, and lips until you reach 11, your birth date. The forehead means you are smart; the eyes, good-looking; the nose, nosy; and the lips, a good kisser. If you were born on the 11th of a month, you are nosy. Congratulations!

After you figure your fortune feel free to change the categories. The forehead could mean you would be a scientist; the eyes, a photographer; the nose, a baker; and the lips, a singer. For variety, change the body parts, substituting chin, ears, cheeks, and top of head and coming up with a fortune for each one. Continue using the birth date to tell the fortune.

Hippity Hopscotch

Number of players: 2 or more
Location: Outside
Energy level: Lively

Type of game: Balancing
Equipment: Sidewalk chalk
and a small stone

Hippity hop, do not stop. Grab a piece of chalk, find a driveway or sidewalk, and draw the hopscotch blocks as shown in the picture you see here. You're ready to go. The object of this game is to hop on the hopscotch squares to the end and return to the beginning. All players gather behind square 1. The first player hops on one foot on blocks 1, 2, and 3; on two feet on blocks 4 and 5; back to one foot on block 6; on two feet on blocks 7 and 8; on one foot on block 9; and then lands on both feet in the curved area also known as 10. Then, the player jumps up with both feet and turns around in the air, landing in the same place but facing toward the start. Every player takes a turn doing this.

For a challenge, have each player find a stone. The object of this version is to skip over the block you've tossed the stone into on the way up to the curved area, number 10. You have to go in order starting with block 1. What this means is that you play as before, but you must not hop in whatever block the stone is in. If it is 6, for example, don't hop on 6; jump from blocks 4 and 5 to blocks 7 and 8, landing with one foot on block 7 and one foot on block 8.

On the way back to square 1, continue to hop, stopping in the square right before the square with the stone in it. Bend down, pick up the stone, and hop in that square and proceed to square 1. You are out if you fail to throw the stone in the correct square or lose your balance and fall down. If the stone lands on the line between two number blocks, throw again. If it lands between the number blocks again, you have to wait for another turn. Continue to play, watch your balance, and become a hippity hopscotch wiz.

Teddy Bear Pass

Number of players: 2 or more
Location: Indoors or Outdoors
Equipment: A medium-size stuffed animal

Energy level: Lively
Type of game: Balancing

Teddy bear, teddy bear, turn around. Teddy bear, teddy bear, don't fall to the ground. If you do not have a medium-size stuffed animal, a beach ball also works well.

The object of this game is to take your bear, put it underneath your chin, and pass it to your friend without using your hands. Your friend passes it back. Now put the bear between your knees and pass it without dropping it.

If you've mastered this, try standing side by side with your partner, shoulder to shoulder, and put the bear between your shoulders. Can you walk, run, or skip while holding it there? What about standing back to back or head to head with the bear between you?

If you have more than one pair of players, have everyone line up, side by side, shoulder to shoulder, with a bear between each pair of players' shoulders. On the count of three, start walking. How far can you go? How fast?

What's Missing?

Number of players: 2 or more
Location: Indoors
Equipment: Items on the kitchen table

Energy level: Calm
Type of game: Guessing

How good is your memory? Gather around the kitchen table and look to see what is on it. Only a few items? Add something you might use at a meal, such as salt and pepper shakers, napkins, candles, place mats, silverware, a sugar bowl, or anything else meal-related. The object of this game is to remove an item from the table and see if a selected player notices.

Choose one player to close his eyes. A second player removes an object and places it in her lap or out of sight. Tell the first player to open his eyes. Can he guess what is missing? Take turns. Want a change? Add something to the table and see if it is noticed.

This game is also entertaining at a restaurant. Dinner will come a lot sooner than you expected.

Get Up!

Number of players: 2 or any even number,
   played in pairs
Location: Indoors or Outdoors

Equipment: None
Energy level: Calm
Type of game: Balancing

This game is guaranteed to provide lots of laughs and silly acrobatics. Play in pairs either on the carpet or outside on the grass. The object of this game is to get up from a sitting position to a standing position. If you think it sounds easy, try it!

First, you and your partner sit on the ground, back to back, legs stretched out, arms linked at the elbow. Then, raise your knees and try to get up from the ground without breaking the link or using your hands.

Here are some tips: Sit as straight as you can, push against each other's back as hard as you can, and try to stand up. It may take several times, but don't give up. Alternatively, both of you can lean to one side and one of you try to get to your knees using your elbows to help. Then, if you can, lift your partner up as you stand up.

Maybe you'll come up with your own method—give it a go and Get Up!

Tabletop Hockey

Number of players: 2 or more, played 2 at a time
Location: Indoors

Equipment: A table, a nickel, a penny, and a dime
Energy level: Lively
Type of game: Strategy

Your fingers are hockey sticks and three coins—a penny, a nickel, and a dime—are the pucks. This game is played by two at a time, with players sitting at opposite ends of the table. The object of this game is to shoot the puck between two goals. Flip the penny to see who starts. The winner of the toss takes the three coins and lines them up at her end of the table in this order: penny, dime, nickel. Others can join in by playing the winner of a round.

The penny is the first puck and your index finger is the hockey stick. To begin, put your index finger on the penny and shoot it out onto the center of the table. Next, shoot the dime. Try not to shoot too far, the penny and the dime become the temporary goalposts. The next move is to shoot the nickel between the penny and dime. This creates a new goal whose goalposts are the penny and the nickel. Shoot the dime between the two. Play continues always in this order toward the other end of the table.

As the action is moving toward the end of the table, your opponent makes goalposts at the end of the table using only his index fingers and thumbs; the other fingers are folded under. He rests his index fingers on the top of the table while his thumbs touch the edge of the table, with the remaining three fingers folded under, forming the goal.

At this point you are trying to shoot a goal into the goalpost fingers. If you shoot and miss, your turn is over and it is your opponent's turn. If you win, you start over again. Switch turns if you win three times in a row. Wayne Gretzky, look out.

Leapfrog

Number of players: 2 or any even number, played in pairs
Location: Outdoors

Equipment: None
Energy level: Lively
Type of game: Racing

The object of this classic game is to leap over the frog in front of you. One player, acting like a frog, kneels down on the ground and tucks his head in front of his knees, cradling his head with his hands. His partner stands behind the frog, lightly touches his back, leaps over him, and crouches down in front of him in the starting position. He immediately gets up and leaps over his partner. Play continues until a player falls over or reaches the end of an agreed-upon line.

Got a lot of players? Divide into teams and set start and finish lines about 100 steps apart. Race each other. Acrobatic amphibians absolutely!

Miss Sue from Alabama

Number of players: 4 or more
Location: Outdoors
Equipment: None

Energy level: Calm
Type of game: Clapping

This is a musical clapping game played standing in a circle using a musical rhyme, "Miss Sue from Alabama."

> *Miss Sue, Miss Sue, Miss Sue from Alabama*
> *Sitting in a rocking chair*
> *Eating a barrel of crackers*
> *Watching the clock go tick, tock, tick, tock, finale nally*
> *go tick, tock, tick, tock, finale nally*
> *A B C D E F G wash those cooties off of me*
> *Mucho mucho mucho freeze!*

The object of this game is to sing the rhyme while making movements that match the meaning of each line. To start, each person puts her arms out to the sides, elbows bent and palms up. Each player places the back of her right hand on top of the palm of the player to the right, and her left hand underneath the hand of the player to the left. In rhythm, perform the following motions:

ON FIRST LINE: One player begins by bringing her right arm over to the player on her left and tapping her right palm to that player's right palm. The next player does the same thing, and so on, until everyone has clapped the hand of the person on her left.

ON SECOND LINE: All players make fists and clasp them to their chests and rock back and forth on their feet.

ON THIRD LINE: All players bring their fingers to their mouths and pretend to be feeding themselves crackers.

ON FOURTH AND FIFTH LINES: Players put their hands together in front of them and move them side to side on the *tick, tock*s like the pendulum of a clock. On the *finale nally*, players put their hands up and wiggle their fingers.

ON SIXTH LINE: Players pretend to wash themselves by using their hands to rub their arms.

ON SEVENTH LINE: Repeat the clapping motion from the first line but try not to have your palm be the one tapped on the word *freeze* or you are out.

This game continues in rounds until there is only one player left.

Germ Buster

Number of players: 5 or more
Location: Outdoors
Equipment: A medium-size ball

Energy level: Action-packed
Type of game: Tagging

Who you gonna call? Germ Buster! Dodging, ducking, chasing, and busting are a few of the skills required to play this game. The object is to tag/bust the player/germ holding the ball.

Choose one member of the group to be the germ buster. All other players are called germs. Define the playing area. Then form a circle of germs with the germ buster in the middle holding the ball.

On the count of three, the germ buster throws the ball up in the air and all players scatter. The germ buster must catch the ball and try to tag any player by throwing the ball at him below his waist. If the ball touches above the waist, it does not count. Once a germ has been tagged, he sits down. He can be freed and rejoin the game if a fellow germ tags his shoulder. Play continues until the germ buster has busted all the germs.

Picture This

Number of teams: 2 teams of at least 2
Location: Indoors or Outdoors
Energy level: Lively

Equipment: Indoors, 2 pieces of paper and crayons. Outdoors, chalk
Type of game: Relay

This is a creative relay game. The object is for your team to create a picture before the other team does.

Divide the group into 2 equal teams. After you have decided whether to play inside or outside, set up the end lines at least 20 feet apart. Put your materials at one end of the playing area. The teams line up at the other end. Decide on the subject to be drawn, such as a person, a house, or an animal.

At the count of three, the first player of each team races to the art supplies and begins drawing the initial shape of the object, such as a circle for a face. After completing her part, she puts the chalk or crayon down and returns to the end of her team's line. Each player in turn adds one key item to the picture. For a face this might be an eye, a nose, an ear, or hair. The game continues with 4 turns per player. The team that finishes first wins. Can you picture this?

Cat and Mouse

Number of players: 4 or more
Location: Outdoors
Equipment: A bandanna or scarf

Energy level: Lively
Type of game: Running

Catch me if you can, you crazy cat. The classic Marco Polo game, but this one is played on land. The object of this game is to catch the mouse while blindfolded.

Set up a clear, confined, safe playing area, like the front yard with no objects to get in the way (such as toys, bikes, lawn furniture, or equipment). Choose one player to be the cat and blindfold him. A bandanna or scarf is an ideal blindfold. All other players are mice.

One mouse spins the cat around three times. After the third spin all the mice run around and never stop moving. The cat then tries to catch any mouse. To do this, the cat says "meow, meow." The mice must respond wherever they are by saying "squeak, squeak." The first mouse to be caught becomes the next cat.

The Wishing Box

Number of players: 2 or any even number, played in pairs

Location: Indoors or Outdoors

Equipment: Paper and pencil for both players

Energy level: Calm

Type of game: Arts/Imagination

I wish I may, I wish I might have the wish I wish right now. The object of this game is create a wishing box with a partner and find out if your wishes will come true. Get a piece of paper and a pencil and have one person draw a square. Next divide the square into four equal parts. Number the squares 1 through 4. Now ask your partner these questions and record the answers in the boxes:

1. *If you could have any toy what would it be?*
   Write the first letter of the toy in box 1.
2. *What is your favorite number?*
   Write the number in box 2.
3. *What is your favorite letter?*
   Write the letter in box 3.

In box 4 draw a heart and say, "I am going to make your wish come true. This heart seals your wish." If box 1 had a *B* for baseball, and box 2 had the number 20, and box 3 had an *M,* for example, the wish would go like this: You will get a baseball on the twentieth of a month from Michael (the name of someone both players know that begins with the chosen letter).

Change roles and let your partner become the wish giver. When you have each granted a few toy wishes, try creating your own categories: who you will marry, the day, and how many children you will have; what you will be when you grow up, and what state you will live in, what will be your lucky number, etc.

Another way to play is to grant the wish giver the opportunity to interpret the wisher's choice of letters and numbers and thus the wish. Play follows the same order. The wish giver has the fun of making up the wisher's favorite toy, number, and letter. For example, the wisher may have been thinking baseball, 20, and Michael, but the wish giver translates the first letters of these items in to other possibilities, such as basketball, 12, and Matthew.

The Rename Game

Number of players: 2 or more
Location: Indoors or Outdoors
Equipment: None

Energy level: Calm
Type of game: Arts/Imagination

Do you want to change your name? The object of this game is for each player in turn to take the first letter of their name and think of three new names beginning with that letter. The first name must be funny, the second a nonsense word, and the third a boy's name if you are a girl and a girl's name if you are a boy. For example, Chelsea could become Chompers for a funny name, Calalula for a nonsense name, and Charlie for a boy's name. Fran could become Frisbee, Feripta, and Fred. Do you like any of the names you came up with better than the real one?

Freeze Tag

Number of players: 5 or more
Location: Outdoors
Equipment: None

Energy level: Action-packed
Type of game: Tagging

This is a classic tag game enjoyed by a group. The object is for the player who is chosen to be It to tag and thereby freeze all players. Settle on a playing area, such as the backyard, and set your boundaries. Choose a player to be It. Play begins after It has counted to three.

When It tags someone, the tagged player must freeze in position and stay there unless rescued by another player. A player who is not frozen can tag her on the shoulder to unfreeze her.

To make it more difficult, add a step to the rescuing process. When a player tags a frozen player on the shoulder to defrost her, the frozen player must immediately crawl through her rescuer's legs. This takes a bit more time and both players run the risk of being tagged and frozen.

In both versions it is important to set a time limit, such as 5 to 10 minutes. The game ends when the time limit has expired. Start a new round.

Corny Costume Relay

Number of teams: 2 teams of at least 3
Location: Indoors or Outdoors
Equipment: Variety of items of clothing and accessories
Energy level: Action-packed
Type of game: Relay

How corny can you look in the shortest amount of time? Gather a variety of clothing and accessories from around your house, such as a baseball cap and glove, old shoes, scarves, bike helmets, costume jewelry, dresses, and pants. Use your imagination. The object of this game is to be the first team to complete the relay.

Decide on start and finish lines, about 20 feet apart. Divide the costume items into two piles; take them to the finish line. As there will be two teams, place one pile in one spot, the other in a spot 5 feet away. Line up the teams at the start line. On the count of three, the first player on each team races to the pile of clothes and as quickly as possible puts on everything in the pile. Once dressed, she runs back to the next player in line on her team, tags his hand, then runs back to the finish line and takes off the corny costume. She races back to the start line and tags the same player, who runs down and puts on the corny costume and repeats the running and tagging sequence.

For a twist and some laughs, truly mix up how the costume is put together. Shoes go on hands, coats on heads, scarves around knees, dresses on backward. Ham it up, be as corny as you can.

Chain Tag

Number of players: 6 or more
Location: Outdoors
Equipment: None

Energy level: Action-packed
Type of game: Tagging

The object of this school-yard favorite is to tag all the players and create a human chain. Decide on the playing area, for example, the front yard. Pick a site for the base, maybe the front steps, which will be the safe area where a player cannot be tagged. Choose someone to be It.

To start, all players spread out and It chases and tags a player. Once tagged, a player links arms with It. As a twosome, each end can tag. The next player tagged immediately links arms with the person who tagged her, creating a longer chain and becoming one of the ends, free to tag another player. The chain can move in any direction, but it is important that all players move together. At any time, a player can run to base to escape being tagged. The game ends when the chain includes all players.

Zip Zap Zop

Number of players: 4 or more
Location: Indoors or Outdoors
Equipment: None

Energy level: Calm
Type of game: Racing

Zip, zap, zop, how fast can you go? The object of this game is to play as fast as you can and stay in the game.

To start, everyone stands in a circle. One player says "zip" while pointing his index finger at another player. That player, in turn, says "zap" while pointing to yet another player. The third player says "zop" while pointing to any other player. Players continue by pointing and saying "zip," then "zap," then "zop." A player can point to whomever he chooses. A player is out if he doesn't say the correct word in sequence or say it in rhythm. The laughter erupts as the speed of the game increases.

Spin Search

Number of players: 4 or more,
    played 2 at a time
Location: Outdoors

Equipment: None
Energy level: Lively
Type of game: Hunting

Can you find me after you have spun around three times with your eyes closed? This game is played in twos; the object of this game is to dizzily find your fellow player while keeping your eyes shut. Other players stand on the sidelines watching and waiting for the next round.

Agree on your playing area. It should be medium-size and free of objects that a player might trip over. Select one player who chooses a spot in the playing area and stands still. The other player moves away at least 20 feet, shuts his eyes, and spins around three times with his eyes closed at all times. At the end of the last spin, eyes still shut, he puts his arms out as bumpers while he tries to locate the silent player, who is not allowed to move. The challenge is to find the player quickly without any help from the other players. When he locates the player, he moves to the sideline and the caught player chooses someone to come in to play. Continue in rounds, each round rotating a new player into the game.

To broaden the game, you can add objects to be found such as a basketball pole, a garbage can, a tree, or an outdoor chair. Continue as before and search away.

Watch Out

Number of players: 3 or more
Location: Outdoors
Equipment: A large soft ball

Energy level: Lively
Type of game: Dodging

A large soft ball (such as the kind sold in supermarkets and drugstores) and the side of the house or a garage door are all you need to play this game.

Line the players up 15 to 20 feet from the wall (the side of the house or the garage door). Choose one player to be It, who will be the first one to throw the ball.

On the count of three, It throws the ball up in the air and waits to catch it while the other players run to the wall. The object of this game is to reach the wall before being tagged below the waist by the ball. If the ball tags above the waist, the player is free. The player tagged is the next one to throw the ball. Watch out!

THIRD AND FOURTH GRADE:
Eager Beavers

No-List Scavenger Hunt

Number of players or teams: 2 or more
(if more, play in teams)
Location: Indoors or Outdoors
Equipment: Indoors, paper and pencil
for each player
Outdoors, none

Energy level:
Lively
Type of game:
Hunting

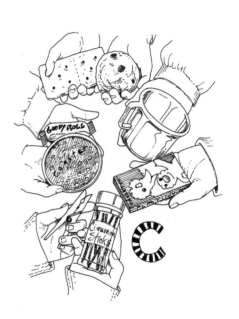

The hunt is on, but what are we hunting for? That's what's great about this game. Unlike the traditional scavenger hunt, which requires a lot of planning, this version is quite easy and adaptable. The object is to be the first player or team to gather the necessary items. Decide on a category to collect and the number of things to be collected. Increase the number in each new round as the excitement builds.

What could you collect? A good starting point might be 10 different treasures. If it's a beautiful day, why not start outside collecting 10 green or brown nature objects or 5 green and 5 brown. Other items to find might include types of seashells, items that begin with a particular letter, any types of seeds, or flower petals. For variety, the first player or team finished collecting has to construct something with them, such as an art display.

This works well indoors too, just change what you are hunting for. So that your house isn't turned upside down, give every player a pencil and paper to write down the objects they find and where they are located. To start, why not collect red or blue items, books with titles beginning with the letter *J*, foods, or anything that relates to the family pet. Another variation is to give each player or team an old magazine and a pair of scissors to cut out the items being hunted.

Menu Madness

Number of players: 3 or more
Location: Indoors
Equipment: Menus for take-out food

Energy level: Calm
Type of game: Strategy

Let's have some fun with the take-out menus lying around your kitchen. The object of this game is to answer questions about a menu. Choose one. Look it over, check it out, and answer a few simple questions. What have you never heard of before? What sounds the grossest? What's the most expensive item? What's the least expensive? What would you order if you had just arrived back from being stranded on a desert island for a year? Take it from here and create your own menu madness queries.

Hand Jive

Number of players: 2 or any even number, played in pairs
Location: Indoors or Outdoors

Equipment: None
Energy level: Lively
Type of game: Tapping

Hand jive alive, fists are tapping, words are slapping. Use your imagination to think of compound words, two words that make one, such as baseball, snowflake, or playroom. The object of this game is for both players in a pair to tap out a simple eight-beat hand rhythm together while saying their word. The movement goes like this:

Each player makes fists with both hands;

Player 1 taps the bottom of his fists to the top of player 2's fists twice saying "hand jive," one word per action.

Each player opens his hands and player 1 gently slaps his

palms to player 2's palms twice while player 1 says his chosen word (for example, snowflake) during each movement;

Players again tap fists bottom to top twice, again saying "hand jive."

Each player then opens his hands and player 1 gently slaps the back of his hands to player 2's backs twice while player 2 says his word (for example, baseball) during each movement.

Pick a partner. Each player chooses a word, starts the rhythm. How many times can you do it? How fast can you hand-jive?

Backward Ho

Number of players: 1 or more
Location: Indoors
Equipment: Paper, pencil, and a cup

Energy level: Calm
Type of game: Backward

Everything seems so simple until you do it backward. This is a great activity to try by yourself or with your friends. The object is to do everything backward. All you need is a piece of paper and a pencil. Start by saying the alphabet backward. If you think you are good, time yourself. Next, try writing 1 to 25. Try it in reverse. How about writing your first and last name backward.

Got this under control? Go for something more advanced. Sit on the floor and put the paper behind you. Try drawing a star. Now a person. Keep going, each time choosing something different to draw. Can you write your name behind your back backward?

Now for some action. Hop backward 10 hops. Try drinking water from the back of a cup while kneeling. Be adventurous and see what you can come up with.

Backward ho, you're the pro. Say a sentence backward. For example, "Mom, may I please have some milk?" would translate to "Milk some have please I may, Mom." If you master this, try having a conversation. Ho Backward!

TV Tag

Number of players: 5 or more
Location: Outdoors
Equipment: None

Energy level: Action-packed
Type of game: Tagging

This classic tag game was developed with the advent of television. The object of this game is to avoid being tagged by shouting out the name of a TV show.

Set the boundaries of the playing area. The person who is It must be someone whose name starts with the letter in the alphabet closest to *T* or *V* for TV.

This tag centers on old and new TV programs. If a player is about to be tagged by It, all he has to do is kneel down and shout out the name of a TV show. If he does this and is not challenged about the accuracy of the name, he is safe. If he is challenged and is incorrect or cannot name a TV show or does not kneel down, he is the next It.

For variety, try movies. You can also use CD or book titles.

Candy Socks Relay

Number of teams: 2 teams of at least 4
Location: Indoors or Outdoors
Equipment: 3 pieces of wrapped candy for
each player and 2 pairs of socks

Energy level: Lively
Type of game: Relay

This game is silly and sweet. It is tough to complete, but the reward can't be beat. Find 2 pairs of thick, clean socks and at least 3 pieces of wrapped candy per player. These sweets could be chocolate, peppermints, or sourballs. Divide the group into 2 equal teams and sit in separate circles with the socks and the candy in the middle of each circle.

The object of this relay is to put the socks on your hands and unwrap a piece of candy. The game is played in rounds. The first team to finish 3 rounds wins. On the count of three, one player from each team puts the socks on and takes a piece of candy from the center. The player unwraps the candy as quickly as possible and eats it. Then she takes off the socks and passes them right side out to the player on the left. That player repeats the action. If your candy source is unlimited, and your mom says it's okay, keep going in rounds. You can decide how many. Just remember to have enough pieces of candy for all players.

Crab Walk

Number of players or teams: 4 or more
  (if more, play in teams)
Location: Indoors on carpet or
  Outdoors on grass

Equipment: None
Energy level: Lively
Type of game: Balancing

How does a crab walk? This game uses your knees, so it is best played on carpet or grass. Choose a leader. Get down on your knees and form a line one player behind another. Grab the ankles of the player in front of you and begin the crab walk. The object of this game is to move around in a line. How far can you go? How fast can you go without breaking the link? Feeling competent? Try going in circles, from room to room, or all around the yard.

If you have lots of players, form 2 equal teams. Set start and finish lines about 20 feet apart. Which team can get to the end first? Now set up an obstacle course with whatever is around you, such as lawn furniture, stuffed animals, books, or pillows. Be as innovative as possible with your course.

Try crab-walking solo. Sit on the ground, knees up. Put your arms behind you, planting your palms on the ground. Now lift your body up by pushing on your palms. Can you move forward? Can you move backward? After you have practiced a little, try a race or an obstacle course. Crab-walk away!

Monkey in the Middle

Number of players: 4 or more
Location: Outdoors
Equipment: A ball

Energy level: Action-packed
Type of game: Tossing

This is the classic keep-away game. Gather in a circle and have one player, the monkey, stand in the middle. The object is to throw the ball over, around, or through the monkey's legs to another player without letting the monkey intercept the ball. If the monkey catches the ball, the person who threw it is now in the middle as the monkey.

To make the game more difficult, add this rule: If the person receiving the ball does not catch it or drops it, she becomes the monkey.

Watch out for the monkey in the middle.

Human Knot

Number of players: 4 to 6
Location: Outdoors
Equipment: None

Energy level: Lively
Type of game: Strategy

You know how tough it is to untie a double shoelace knot. Well try a human knot.

The object of this game is to undo the human knot.

Players stand in a circle and on the count of three, join hands. There is one rule: Players can join only one hand with the person on either side. The other hand has to be joined with someone farther away in the circle. Once all hands are linked, everyone takes a step forward to the center of the circle and raises their linked hands in the air. Together, all players twist around, creating a human knot. The challenge begins. Try to untie this human knot. Anything goes but don't let go of any hands (it is okay to rotate the grip) or the knot has to start over. It's important to talk to one another to solve this knotted human loop.

Double Double This This!

Number of players: 2 or any even number, played in pairs

Location: Indoors

Equipment: None

Energy level: Lively

Type of game: Clapping

This is a double doozy of a game for two people. Once you learn the basic rhyme and hand action, the art is in the speed. The rhyme goes like this:

> *Double double this this*
> *Double double that that*
> *Double this*
> *Double that*
> *Double double this that*

The movements go as follows:

ON FIRST LINE: Bend your elbows and make fists with both hands. On the first word *double*, tap the sides of your fists to your partner's sides of fists. Repeat this motion on the second word *double*. On the word *this*, open your fists and tap the backs of your hands to your partner's. Repeat for the second word *this*.

ON SECOND LINE: Repeat the same action for both *double* words. For the word *that*, open your fists and tap your palms to your partner's palms.

ON THE THIRD LINE: Repeat the same action once for the word *double.* On the word *this,* open your fists and tap the backs of your hands together.

ON THE FOURTH LINE: Repeat the same action once for the word *double.* On the word *this,* open your fists and tap your palms together.

ON THE FIFTH LINE: Repeat the same action for both *double* words. On the word *this,* open your fists and tap the backs of your hands together. On the word *that,* tap your palms together.

How fast can you go? Can you do it with only one hand? If there is more than one twosome and your confidence level is high, gather in a circle. Each player will be saying the same rhyme but tapping hands with the player on the right and the player on the left.

Shoe Spin

Number of players: 2 or more
Location: Outdoors
Energy level: Lively

Equipment: Shoes you are wearing and a target
Type of game: Tossing

A simple outdoor game that can be played in your yard, at the park, or on the beach. Gather your friends and make sure everyone is wearing shoes or sandals.

All players stand in a line, side by side. The object is to spin one shoe off your foot, hoping it lands the farthest distance.

A few tips: First choose a foot to shoe-spin and loosen your shoe, removing the heel of your foot from the back of the shoe. The first person in the line starts the shoe spin and players continue one by one. On your turn, stand on the leg you are not shoe-spinning and bring the other foot back with your shoe hanging on your toes. Now, shoe-spin away. Whose shoe went the farthest?

Mastered the art of shoe spinning? Find a target such as a bucket, hula hoop, Frisbee, or towel. Who can spin his shoe onto the target?

Mirror Writing

Number of players: 1 or more
Location: Indoors
Equipment: A mirror, paper, and pencil

Energy level: Calm
Type of game: Strategy

Mirror, mirror on the wall, what do I see? An engaging activity for the detective in all of us. The object of this game is to write a word, phrase, or sentence backward so that it can be read correctly when held in front of a mirror (a bathroom mirror works great).

Notice that when you write any phrase or sentence on paper, it's simple to read. If you hold that piece of paper in front of a mirror, however, it is unreadable. How can you write it so you can read it in the mirror? Four simple steps:

Step 1:   Choose a phrase   Example: ☛ Hey Mom, I'm Bored!

Step 2:   Reverse the order of the words   Example: ☛ !Bored I'm, Mom Hey
           and punctuation.

Step 3:   Reverse the order of letters   Example: ☛ !deroB m'I, moM yeH
           in each word.

Step 4:   Reverse the direction of each letter   Example: ☛ Hey Mom, I'm Bored!
           and the comma.

You will notice that some printed lower-case letters look the same when you reverse them, such as i,l,o,t,v,w, and x.

If you are by yourself, test this out. Try writing your first and last name and address. Feeling like you've mastered mirror writing? Why not write a mirror message to your mom and dad. Can they understand it? Can they decode it? If you have a pen pal, mirror-write a whole letter. Don't forget to give a clue how to read the letter (that is, hold it up to a mirror).

If you are with a friend, look through a newspaper, magazine, or book. Choose a short paragraph and see which one of you can successfully mirror-write it so that it is readable in the mirror.

Surprise Jar

Number of players: 4 or more
Location: Indoors or Outdoors
Equipment: A medium-size jar, paper,
  and pencil

Energy level: Lively
Type of game: Laughing

Surprise, surprise! What will you have to do? The object of this game is to perform the activity selected from the jar.

Have everyone sit in a circle. Choose one player to start. He writes a whimsical activity on the piece of paper, then tears off the activity, folds it up, puts it in the surprise jar, and passes the pencil and paper to the next player. Each player contributes an activity. Then the first player picks a piece of paper from the jar and follows the instructions. If a player chooses his own slip, it is okay to perform the activity.

Some of the activities might include:

- Do 10 jumping jacks.
- Say the alphabet backward.
- Walk backward as you spell your name backward.
- Sing your favorite song.
- Do a cartwheel or a donkey kick.
- Put your shoes on the opposite feet and do a tapdance.

- Touch your tongue to your nose.
- Hop on one foot while saying everybody's name.
- Pat your head and rub your tummy while walking backward.

See what you can invent so others will be surprised!!

Mr. Mars and His Stars

Number of players: 6 or more
Location: Outdoors
Equipment: None

Energy level: Action-packed
Type of game: Tagging

A marvelous game for a multitude outside. Choose one person to be Mr. Mars for a boy or Mrs. Mars for a girl. The other players are stars. Outline your playing field, the backyard, for example. Mr. Mars stands in the middle of the playing area while the stars line up at one end. The object of this game is for the stars to run to the other end of the playing field without being tagged by Mr. Mars.

The group of stars calls out, "Mr. Mars, may we pass right through your stars?" Mr. Mars chooses a trait, such as blond hair, and says "Yes, if you have blond hair, Go!" If Mr. Mars tags a star running to the opposite end, the star stays exactly where she was tagged and can tag and freeze other stars as they try to pass by.

If a star makes it to the other side, she waits until the rest of the untagged stars join her. Then Mr. Mars turns around and faces that group and selects another distinguishing characteristic such as baseball caps, black shoes, silver rings, sports watches, striped shirts, blue jean shorts, or red bathing suits. The game continues from one end to the other until all the stars have been tagged. The last player tagged is the new Mr. Mars.

Go, Mr. Mars and stars!

Push Button Forecast

Number of players: 2 or any even number, played in pairs
Location: Indoors or Outdoors
Equipment: An 8½″ × 11″ piece of paper and a pencil

Energy level: Calm
Type of game: Guessing

Want to know your favorite sport, who you will marry, your lucky number, your best friend, or your favorite music? By pushing the buttons you are about to make, you can forecast the future for a friend.

Step 1: Fold the piece of paper in half (top to bottom), then in half again (top to bottom). Now hold it with your left hand and fold the right side over to the left side. Open the paper up. There should be 8 boxes created by the folds and 2 vertical columns each containing 4 boxes. Each box will be labeled.

Step 2: In the top left-hand box, write *Push Button Forecast.*

Step 3: At the top of the box below Push Button Forecast, write *Sports.* Draw 6 lines and number each line. On each line, write a sport, for example, skiing, swimming, soccer, basketball, baseball, and tennis.

Step 4: At the top of the box below Sports, write *Lucky Number.* Draw 6 lines and number each line. On each line, write a lucky number, for example, 25, 43, 9, 81, 36, and 5.

Step 5: In the bottom box on the left side, write *Music.* Draw 6 lines and number each line. On each line, write the name of a musical group, for example, 'N SYNC, Dixie Chicks, Backstreet Boys, Ricky Martin, Sugar Ray, and Garth Brooks.

Step 6: Move to the top of the page. In the first box on the right-hand side, write *Girls' Marry.* Draw 6 lines and number each line. On each line, write the name of a boy. They can be names of people you know or just names you like. For example, Tony, Michael, Carl, John, Drew, and Jay.

Step 7: At the top of the box below Girls' Marry, write *Boys' Marry.* Draw 6 lines and number each line. On each line, write the name of a girl. Again, they can be names of people you know or just names you like. For example, Maggie, Abby, Chelsea, Madeleine, Fee, and McCrea.

Step 8: At the top of the box below Boys' Marry, write *Girls' Best Friend.* Draw 6 lines and number each line. On each line, write the name of a girl. For example, Anne, Vicki, Sandie, Katie, Judy, and Connie.

Step 9: At the top of the bottom box on the right side, write *Boys' Best Friend*. Draw 6 lines and number each line. On each line, write the name of a boy. For example, Peter, Casey, Bill, Ryan, Allen, Rob.

Step 10: Fold the paper up again, the way you did to start, ending with a small rectangle. On that rectangle, write *Push* and draw a circle representing a button. Open up the paper once so it is a long narrow rectangle (really two of the boxes). In the left box, write *Girl* and in the right box, write *Boy*. Draw 2 buttons, one under Girl and one under Boy.

Step 11: Open the paper so it is folded in half. On one side, write *Girl* and on the other side, write *Boy*. Under both Girl and Boy write the categories: Sports, Marriage, Lucky Number, Best Friend, and Favorite Music. Draw a button for each category.

Step 12: Let the forecasting begin. Fold up the square as in step 10 and ask your friend to push the button to start. Next, open up the paper and have her push the Girl button since she is a girl. Unfold the paper again and ask her to push one of the category buttons, such as Music. Ask her to pick a number between 1 and 6. She picks 5. Open the paper all the way and go to Music. Sugar Ray is her favorite.

Continue in the same way for each category. There will be lots of laughs and giggles when you forecast the future. Now, have your friend forecast your future. For variety, change the topics. Examples might be States Live In, Favorite Color, Favorite Food, Careers, Age Marry, Girls' Favorite Clothing Store, and Boys' Favorite Baseball Player.

Potato Race

Number of teams: 2 teams of at least 2
Location: Outdoors
Equipment: For each player: a potato or
   round fruit and a spoon

Energy level: Action-packed
Type of game: Relay

This is a classic team relay game with many ways to play. The object is to be the first team to race your potato down to the finish line and back to the start line. In all versions a potato or round fruit is required for each team, and in one version a spoon is needed for each team. If you do not have a potato, use an apple, orange, or grapefruit. Play with as many potato pals as you can find.

The best-known version is a relay race using a spoon. Set start and finish lines, about 20 feet apart. Teams line up at the start line, each with a potato on a spoon. At the count of three, players must run to the finish line, cross it, and then run back to the start line without dropping the potato. If the potato falls off the spoon, the player must pick it up with the spoon and continue. Once back at the start line, pass the spoon and potato to the next player on the team. The team who finishes first wins.

In the second version, players put the potato between their knees and hold it there. On the count of three, each team's player runs to the finish line, crosses it, and then runs back to the start line without losing the potato. If the potato falls to the ground, the player picks it up, puts it back between his knees, and keeps going. Once a player has finished his turn, he passes the potato to the next team member. The team who finishes first wins.

The third version begins with each team's potato on the ground at the start line. On the count of three, the first player on each team bends down and tries to scoop the potato up and place it under his chin, using no hands. This is not an easy feat, but once it has been accomplished, players race to the finish line, cross it, and return to the start line. The first team done wins.

The toughest version uses any part of the head and no hands. Place each team's potato on the ground at the start line. On the count of three, the first player on each team lies face down on the ground behind her potato. The object is to crawl and push the potato using nose, chin, cheek, or forehead to the finish line and then back to the start line. The first potato head wins.

Flying George

Number of players: 2 or more
Location: Indoors or Outdoors
Equipment: Dollar bill for each player

Energy level: Lively
Type of game: Throwing/Catching

Do you know who is on the one-dollar bill? It's America's first president, George Washington. Find a dollar bill for each player and have the players fold them into airplanes. The object of this game is to fly your plane across the finish line.

Define start and finish lines not too far apart, say about 5 feet. Players take turns and play in rounds. How many times does your plane successfully cross the finish line? Feel free to redesign your airplane at any point. Extend the distance to the finish line as players become more expert in flying.

You can also play this game using a baseball cap as a landing pad for George. The object of this version is to land your plane in the cap.

Puzzle Hunt

Number of teams: 2 teams of at least 2
Location: Outdoors
Equipment: 2 jigsaw puzzles, each with no
more than 40–50 pieces

Energy level: Lively
Type of game: Hunting

Two different jigsaw puzzles are necessary for this game, 40 to 50 pieces work best. It's possible that all the puzzle pieces will not be found during the game, so choose puzzles you wouldn't mind ruining.

Divide into 2 equal teams. Agree on a place to put the puzzles together, such as the driveway. Give each team a puzzle box. Each team selects a player from the opposing team to hide its puzzle pieces. The puzzles are hidden in separate locations, for example, one team's in the front yard and the other team's in the backyard. The object of this game is to find all the hidden puzzle pieces and assemble the jigsaw puzzle before the other team assembles its. If a team ends up with pieces belonging to the other team, it passes them to the other team.

This game has the thrill of a hunt and the excitement of a race. Happy hunting!

Letter Lookout

Number of players: 3 or more
Location: Indoors
Equipment: Paper and pencil for each player

Energy level: Lively
Type of game: Hunting

Stuck inside and can't find anything to do? Try Letter Lookout. The object of this game is to find items around the house to match letters of the alphabet.

You can play two ways. For the first version, each player writes the alphabet down along the left side of the paper. At the count of three, players disperse throughout the house trying to locate items to match each letter of the alphabet. For example, apple for A, baseball for B, *Time* magazine for T, perfume for P, or vacuum for V. All players must write down a found object beginning with each letter and its location.

First one back to the starting place with a completed alphabet yells, "Letter Lookout," which signals all players back. Don't worry, the game may not be over. There is always the possibility that this player made up an item. Together, go through each player's list. Feel free to challenge any item listed, but you can only do this 3 times. If it's discovered that an item does not exist, the game continues but that player is out. For example, if a player lists a flute for F and there's no flute in the house, she is out.

Version two has all players looking for items to match all the letters in a word. The word must be agreed upon by everyone, for example, spaghetti, dictionary, computer, orangutan, or a person's name.

Lots of letters, lots of possibilities.

Three-Legged Kick

Number of players: 4 or any even number, played in pairs

Equipment: For each pair: a ball and a bandanna

Location: Outdoors

Energy level: Action-packed

Type of game: Racing

This is a variation of the classic three-legged race. For each pair of players, find a ball and something to tie ankles with, like a bandanna. The object of this game is to kick the ball from the start to the finish line using only the tied-together legs.

Set the kick start line and the end goal line at least 20 feet apart. Separate into pairs. Stand next to your partner, shoulder to shoulder, and tie your inside ankles together. On the count of three, begin. Kicking sounds simple, but it's not necessarily so. Planning and teamwork make the three-legged kick *click!*

Bola Bola

Number of players: 3 or more
Location: Outdoors
Equipment: A sock, a tennis ball,
   and 4–6 feet of rope

Energy level: Action-packed
Type of game: Jumping

If you like to hop, skip, or jump, this game is for you.

Put the tennis ball in the toe of the sock. Tie one end of the rope (a jump rope is perfect) to the ankle part of the sock. Players stand in a circle. Choose one player to be the twirler, who stands in the center of the circle.

The object of this game is to jump over the spinning rope without it touching your foot or leg. The twirler kneels down and spins the rope around in a circle on the ground while the other players skip or jump over it with both feet. If any part of a player's foot or leg touches the rope, that player sits out. The game ends when there are no players left jumping. Choose a new twirler and begin another round.

If jumping on two feet is too easy, try hopping on one foot. For a new skill, try doing it backward.

FIFTH AND SIXTH GRADE:
Oh, What a Challenge

Capture the Flag

Number of teams: 2 teams of at least 2
Location: Outdoors
Equipment: 2 bandannas, kitchen towels, or baseball caps

Energy level: Action-packed
Type of game: Tagging

All flag runners wanted! The object is to capture the other team's flag without being tagged. First, divide into two teams and find a flag for each team. The flag can be any good-sized cloth object such as a bandanna, kitchen towel, or baseball cap. Decide on the playing field, like the front yard, and divide it in half with an imaginary line that all players agree on. Select a small area on each team's side to be called the jail, where players go if tagged while running on the other team's field.

Start by having each team hide its flag on its side, maybe under a bush or in a tree. Keep a player on guard to make sure that no one from the other team sees where the flag is hidden. To begin, all players reassemble at the centerline. On the count of three, play begins. Team members try to cross to the other side to look for the opponent's flag, capture it, and bring it back to their side without being tagged.

If the enemy tags you, go straight to jail, where you must wait until you are freed. The only way to be freed is to have a teammate cross the border and tag you in jail without being tagged herself. Once a player has been freed, both players are allowed to walk back to their side in peace.

If you are lucky enough to find the flag, capture it and race back to your side. Don't get caught or play starts all over again with you in jail and the flag moved to a new hiding place. This game often lasts for hours and involves many strategy sessions.

Four Square

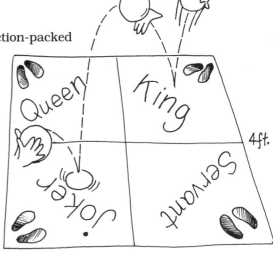

Number of players: 4 or more
Location: Outdoors
Equipment: Sidewalk chalk
   and a medium-size ball

Energy level: Action-packed
Type of game:
   Throwing/
   Catching

Who's square? You're square. We're all square in Four Square. This is a classic outdoor game that requires a piece of chalk and a bouncy medium-size ball such as a basketball, soccer ball, or volleyball. Draw a square about 4 feet by 4 feet and divide it into 4 equal squares. Each square has a name. Starting at the upper right-hand box and going clockwise, label the boxes King, Servant, Joker, and Queen. The order of importance of the positions—king, queen, joker, servant—determines the movement in the game. The object of the game is to stay the king or become the next king by moving up.

Players move to the boxes and the one in the king's square is the first to serve. If you have more than 4 players, the others line up to the side of the servant box.

Play goes as follows. The king serves first, dropping the ball once and then hitting it with his palm to anyone of his choice. That player receives the ball after it has bounced once in her square and hits it to any player of her choice in another square. Play continues until someone misses the ball or it bounces twice in a player's square. If this happens, that player, king, queen, or joker, moves to the servant's square and the other players move up in the hierarchy. If it is the servant who misses, he stays in his square. If there are more than 4 players, the player who missed moves to the end of the line at the side, and the first person waiting in line steps into the servant's box.

It's fast, it's fun, but if you really want to hustle, try these three tactics, which can only be called by the king at the start of each round. The same rules apply, but these relate to how you hit the ball. The first is known as the Cherry Bomb: With great force and speed the king serves the ball to the player of his choice, leaving little time for recovery. However, skilled players, quick on their feet, can often recover and lob the ball to another player. Play continues until someone bombs out.

The Shoeshine directs the ball toward the feet of any player. This calls for some fancy footwork to have enough time and room to let the ball bounce before sending it on its way to the next player's feet. Popcorn adds a slight twist because the ball can never touch the ground: The king serves the ball to a player of his choice, who must stop the ball with her hand and send it on to the next player. Players are not allowed to catch the ball and then throw it.

The king has another trick up his sleeve: At any time when he has the ball, he can call Bus Stop. All players run to the center, where the four squares meet. The king then picks a person to whom the ball will go and shouts out her game position, servant, for example. The servant immediately has to run back to the center of her square to receive the king's ball. Play resumes as before unless the king calls Bus Stop again. Only the king can call Bus Stop.

Guarding Gators

Number of players: 5 or more
Location: Outdoors on grass
Equipment: None

Energy level: Action-packed
Type of game: Tagging

The gators want in and you are the guard of the fortress grounds. The object of this classic game is for the players, called gators, to charge past the guard who is defending his turf.

The guard selects the playing field, such as the backyard, and its boundaries, which must define a grassy area only. The gators line up on their knees at an agreed-upon starting point, about 20 feet away from the guard, who is also on his knees. When the guard yells, "On your mark, get set, go gators," the chase is on. If the guard catches a gator and tags her, that gator helps the guard catch the other gators. The last remaining gator becomes the next guard.

Go, gators!

Who Do You Know Who . . . ?

Number of players: 4 or more
Location: Indoors
Equipment: Paper and pencil for each player

Energy level: Calm
Type of game: Guessing

Who do you know who wears glasses? Who has been to Spain? Who has been to a World Series? Who is a twin? The object of this game is to write a list of questions that can be answered only with the name of someone the player knows personally.

One player is chosen to be the list maker and gives a pencil and piece of paper to everyone. While the other players number their paper 1 to 13, the list maker comes up with thirteen Who Do You Know Who . . . questions such as:

Who Do You Know Who . . .

– has seen Old Faithful?
– can say his or her name in Spanish?
– has eaten chocolate today?
– plays an instrument in an orchestra?
– has a pet mouse?
– has met a U.S. president?
– has three or more brothers or sisters?
– doodles while talking on the phone?
– sleeps with two pillows?
– has a favorite stuffed animal?
– saw a movie in the last week?
– has an autographed baseball?
– had macaroni and cheese for dinner last night?

When the list is complete, play begins. The list maker reads the questions one by one, and as he does the players answer the questions with the names of people they know. If a player does not have a name, she leaves the space blank. After all the questions have been completed, the list maker reads the question and each player in turn reads her answer. Play continues question by question. Players can be challenged as to the authenticity of the person named. The winner or winners (there may be a tie) have the most names and develop the next list of questions. See who you know and what you find out!

Family Magic

Number of players: 2 or more
Location: Indoors or Outdoors
Equipment: Paper and pencil for each player

Energy level: Calm
Type of game: Guessing

This is almost magical. Using this formula, you will be able to identify how many brothers, sisters, and living grandparents a person has in his family.

Choose one person to be the family magician and give all other players a pencil and a piece of paper. The magician asks all players to do the following steps on the paper and to hide all but the final answer.

For example, if one of the players has 1 brother, 3 sisters, and 3 living grandparents, her paper would look like this:

	Example
• Write down number of brothers (1)	1
• Multiply by 2 (1 × 2 = 2)	2
• Add 3 (2 + 3 = 5)	5
• Multiply by 5 (5 × 5 = 25)	25
• Add number of sisters (25 + 3 = 28)	28
• Multiply by 10 (28 × 10 = 280)	280
• Add number of living grandparents (280 + 3 = 283)	283
• Subtract 150 (283 − 150 = 133)	133
• Write down final answer and say it out loud	133

The family magician interprets the number (133) in this order:

- The first number tells the number of brothers you have (1).
- The middle number tells the number of sisters you have (3).
- The last number tells the number of grandparents you have (3).

If the answer is a two-digit number, say 23, put a 0 before the first number, so 23 would become 023. If the answer is a single-digit number, say 3, put 2 zeros before the number, so 3 would become 003. Do this with all single-digit and two-digit numbers.

Have fun dazzling everyone with this family magic.

Hangman

Number of players: 2 or any even number,
  played in pairs
Location: Indoors
Equipment: Paper and pencil
Energy level: Calm
Type of game: Guessing

Find a pencil and a piece of paper and a place to write for this classic word game. The object of this game is to identify a word before a hanging person is completed.

To set up the game, draw an old-fashioned hangman's gallows like the one in this picture. Choose who will be first. That player thinks of a word and draws short lines, one for each letter of the word, below the picture of the gallows. To one side, keep a running list of all the guessed letters that are not used in the word.

The other player must correctly identify the letters in the word and eventually the word itself. On each turn, the guesser says a letter. If the letter is used in the word, the first player writes it on the appropriate short line. If the letter is not part of the word, the first player draws part of a hanging stick-figure body and writes the letter to the side. Start with the head and attach it to the noose. Subsequently add the neck, body, arms, and legs. If you want to stretch the game, feel free to add more detail such as facial features, hands, or feet.

A few hints: Vowels are a good first choice. Start with small words and build up to longer words or phrases, such as man on the moon or Wheel of Fortune. Take turns drawing and guessing.

Skit in a Bag

Number of teams: 2 teams of at least 2
Location: Indoors or Outdoors
Equipment: 2 shopping bags and
   costumes and props

Energy level: Lively
Type of game: Arts/Imagination

You are the producer, Broadway-bound, with a Skit in a Bag. There are no winners or losers, just actors. This is an improvisation game in which players act out any skit they make up using only the costumes and props provided in the bag.

For this team game, use everyday items found in the house. Divide into 2 teams. Find 2 paper or plastic shopping bags. Set a time limit of 10 minutes for teams to collect costumes and props simultaneously. Each team is gathering items for the other team. Some examples might include sunglasses, baseball caps or any other kind of hats, play microphone, clothes from Mom and Dad's closet (get permission first), jewelry, stuffed animals, magazines, scarves, musical instruments, toys, dolls, sports equipment, purses, and shoes.

Select a stage. Swap the bags. Each team moves to separate areas to think through its skit, which will use only the costumes and props in the bag. There is a 10-minute time limit to prepare the skit.

One team goes first, performing for the other. Next, switch and have the other team perform. This activity can be repeated by changing the contents of the bag and mixing up the teams.

Are there Academy Awards in your future?

Tower of Ice

Number of teams: 2 teams of at least 2
Location: Outdoors
Equipment: 2 large bowls of ice cubes
and 2 saltshakers

Energy level: Lively
Type of game: Balancing

A bowl of ice cubes, a shaker of salt, and a warm day are the simple ingredients for Tower of Ice. The object of this game is to see which team can construct the tallest tower of ice in 5 minutes.

Divide the players into 2 teams. Fill 2 large bowls with ice cubes, get 2 saltshakers, and head outdoors. Find a flat area, preferably a driveway, deck, or terrace. Each team lays out its materials. On the count of three, each team begins to build a tower. The salt is used to melt the ice and help the cubes stick together. Experiment with the process to create your tower. Time is up after 5 minutes. Whose tower was the tallest?

For variation, as one group try to create an ice sculpture. Only your imagination limits your possibilities.

Coin Catch

Number of players: 1 or more
Location: Indoors or Outdoors
Equipment: For each player: a quarter,
    a nickel, a dime, and a penny

Energy level: Lively
Type of game: Throwing/Catching

Have you ever flipped a coin and caught it with your hand? That is easy compared to this activity, which uses your elbow. With some practice you can become an expert.

You can do this by yourself or with friends. Start with a quarter and move to a nickel, then to a penny or a dime as you master the art. The object of this game is to catch the coin before it drops to the ground.

Stand and put one arm down at your side. Then bend your elbow so that the back of your thumb touches your shoulder. Raise the elbow up and out to the front so it is level with your shoulder. Cup your hand. Place the quarter 1 inch above your elbow. Quickly move your elbow down toward your hip and try and catch the quarter with the cupped hand.

If you have mastered this, can you coin-catch with the other arm?

Carefully coin-catch!

Passing Perfectly

Number of teams: 2 teams of at least 4

Location: Outdoors

Equipment: 2 plastic cups, dry cereal

Energy level: Lively

Type of game: Racing

Passing perfectly with plastic or paper cups is the aim of this game. The more players, the better.

Get your supplies, 2 cups filled to the brim with dry cereal. Divide the players into 2 teams and line up the teams facing each other about 5 feet apart. The object of this game is to pass the cup quickly from player to player down the line and back, dropping the least amount of cereal. On the count of three, begin.

Want some more fun? Try passing cups filled with water.

The winning team has passed perfectly, ending with the most cereal or water in the cup.

MASH

Number of players: 2 or any even number, played in pairs

Location: Indoors

Equipment: Paper and pencil for each player

Energy level: Calm

Type of game: Guessing

Mansion, Apartment, Shack, or House, do you want to find out where you will live? That is the object of this game. Let's play MASH.

Find a partner, a pencil, and a piece of paper and proceed with the following steps.

Step 1: Think of categories such as food, candy, cars, sports, animals, guys you will marry or girls you will marry, jobs, or colleges. Select 4.

Step 2: At the top of the paper, write the word *MASH*. On the left-hand side of the paper write the first category, say *Food*. Below the category, draw 3 lines and number each line.

In the space below Food, write the next category, such as Cars.

Draw 3 lines and number each line.

In the space below Cars, write the next category, such as Sports.

Draw 3 lines and number each line.

In the space below Sports, write the next category, such as Animals.

Draw 3 numbered lines.

Step 3: Ask your friend to name things to put in the categories. There is a pattern as to how each line is filled: The pattern begins with 2 "hates" and 1 "like" for one category followed by 2 likes and 1 hate for the next category. The pattern repeats itself for the two remaining categories. Don't write the word hate or like, just remember the pattern.

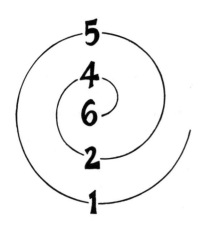

Start with the first category, in this example, Food.

1.	brussels sprouts	(hate)
2.	liver	(hate)
3.	ice cream	(like)

Next category, in this example, Cars.

1.	VW Beetle	(like)
2.	Range Rover	(like)
3.	Cadillac	(hate)

Third category, in this example, Sports.

1.	cross-country	(hate)
2.	field hockey	(hate)
3.	basketball	(like)

Final category, in this example, Animals.

1.	horses	(like)
2.	dogs	(like)
3.	snakes	(hate)

Step 4: On the right-hand side of the paper ask your friend to draw a swirl until she is told to stop. When she stops, count the lines in the swirl, starting from the bottom and going to the top. The beginning of the swirl counts as a line. Let's say your swirl has 5 lines.

Step 5: This next step eliminates lines in each category, until only 4 are left, 1 in each category.

Based on the number of lines in your swirl, in this example 5, you begin at the first line in the first category and count off five. In the example, this would bring you to Range Rover. Strike through it. Starting with the next line, Cadillac, count off five again. This brings you to horses. Strike through it.

In the next set of five, the word MASH is included. MASH is the sixth category. Go from dogs up to MASH. Count off five. Strike through the S. Start counting with the H and move back to the Food category. Five brings you to VW Beetle. Strike through it. Cadillac is left, so circle it.

Start at the Sports category. Count off five. This brings you to snakes. Strike through it, and since there is only one line left, dogs, circle it. Back to MASH and count five. This brings you to liver. Strike through it.

Count off five. This brings you to the M in MASH. Strike through it. Count five again. This brings you to cross-country. Strike through it.

Count off five again. This brings you to brussels sprouts. Strike through it. Ice cream is left, so circle it.

You only have two categories left to work with, Sports and the title MASH. Continue to count off five. This brings you to field hockey. Strike through it and circle basketball. Now only MASH is left. Count off five. This brings you to A. Strike through it and circle the H.

Step 6: Now interpret what is circled. Your friend will live in a house, eat ice cream, drive a Cadillac, play basketball, and have dogs.

Now it is your turn to fill in the categories and draw a swirl. You can vary the categories as you choose. Your life will turn out differently each time.

Dictionary

Number of players: 3 or more
Location: Indoors
Energy level: Lively

Equipment: Paper and pencil for each player and a dictionary
Type of game: Guessing

This is a classic game that tests your knowledge and bluffing skills. The object of this game is to get the most votes for your definition of a word.

Choose one person to be It, the dictionary master. He opens the dictionary, selects what appears to be an uncommon word, and says the word out loud. The object is for all players, including It, to write a definition for that word. It must write the true definition.

For example, if the word is *kowtow,* a real definition is "to be humble in showing obedience and respect." A false whimsical yet possible definition might be "the rope put around a cow's neck to lead it out of a pasture."

All definitions are returned to the dictionary master. It is okay if you do not know the real definition. The aim is to make up a convincing definition.

The dictionary master reads aloud all the definitions including his own. Players vote on which definition is the real one. If your definition has the most votes, regardless of whether it is real or made up, you win a point. Be sure to have the dictionary master read the real definition. You'll be surprised at everyone's creativity and the laughter the definitions incite. Take turns being the dictionary master and continue in rounds. The first player to reach 10 points wins.

Do you know the real definition of *peccadillo?*

Memory Tap

Number of players: 3 or more
Location: Outdoors
Equipment: Items found outside

Energy level: Lively
Type of game: Memory

Like the classic "I Packed My Grandmother's Trunk," this game tests your memory skills, but this one has a twist. This game is played outside using found objects. Items could include a patio table and chairs, an outdoor grill, a garden hose, a flowerpot, a bike, a watering can, an outdoor light, a hula hoop, a ball, rollerblades, and a baseball cap.

To begin, the first player taps an object, such as a hula hoop, says what it is, "hula hoop," and then taps another player. Player 2 taps the first object, the hula hoop, says "hula hoop," taps a new object, such as a flowerpot, says "flowerpot," and then taps another player. Each player in turn repeats the sequence of tapping and saying the previous objects, adds a new object, and then taps a new player. If you cannot remember the correct order of objects or forget one, you are out. Play continues until only one person can remember everything.

Radio Race

Number of players or teams: 2 or more
Location: Indoors
Equipment: A radio

Energy level: Lively
Type of game: Guessing

Do you love music? This game is for you! Tune the radio to your favorite station and play radio race. No winners, no losers, just singers.

The object of this game is to race to name the song title and artist as songs are played. For the final challenge, see if you can sing the whole song.

Radio rocks on!

Shoebox Charades

Number of players: 3 or more
Location: Indoors or Outdoors
Equipment: Paper and pencil for each player
and an empty shoebox

Energy level: Lively
Type of game: Strategy

This game is simply charades but with shoebox rules. Find a shoebox, slips of paper, and a pencil for each player.

Each player writes down on a slip of paper the title of a book, movie, or TV show to be acted out. The slips of paper are put into the shoebox. Players take turns pulling out a slip and acting out their shoebox charade. If you pull out the one you wrote, return it and pick a new one. If someone is acting out your title, don't say what it is, just enjoy the acting. The object is to act out what is on the paper for the group and have the group guess the title within 3 minutes.

Some tips:

Begin by indicating whether it is a TV show, movie, or book: For a TV show, outline a box (like a TV screen) with your fingers. For a movie, pretend to be turning the crank of an old-fashioned movie camera. For a book, put the sides of your hands together, with palms facing up.

The second movement tells the number of words in the title. Hold up as many fingers as there are words in the title. For example, if you are acting out the movie title *My Best Friend's Wedding,* hold out four fingers.

The third action tells the group which word you are working on. Hold up the number of fingers that signifies the place of the word in the title. For example, two fingers would mean the word *Best* in the movie title *My Best Friend's Wedding.*

When trying to indicate a small word like *it, a,* or *the,* show your index finger and thumb with about an inch of space between them.

Once every player has had a turn, start a new round by writing new slips.

Horse Racing

Number of players: 2 or more

Location: Indoors

Equipment: For each player: scissors and a
   sheet of newspaper

Energy level: Lively

Type of game: Racing

You're at the horse races. The gong sounds. The gates open. Charge! Who will win?

A fun racing game involving only newspaper and scissors. Give a page of a newspaper and a pair of scissors to each player. Fold the single page in half lengthwise and cut along the seam fold. Lay one piece on top of the other and again fold in half. Cut along the seam fold. There should now be 4 long, equal pieces of newspaper. Place all the pieces together. At each end make 4 small cuts evenly spaced so that there are 5 equal tabs.

The object of this game is to race your opponents as you tear your 4 individual newspaper pieces as quickly and equally as possible. The first one to tear 20 strips that are complete and equal in size and length wins. Remember you are tearing one strip at a time.

Whoa! This is not as easy as it sounds. Often one strip ends up shorter than the others. This skill takes some practice. Play again and again with new strips each time. Enjoy the races.

Two-Minute Challenge

Number of players: 2 or more
Location: Indoors
Equipment: Paper and pencil for each player

Energy level: Calm
Type of game: Racing

You have 2 minutes to think up items in a category. Choose someone to be the timer. The object of this game is to list in 2 minutes as many items as you can that fit a specified category.

Take turns deciding on a category. Some examples include:

foods that start with *B*
vegetables that grow underground
seafoods that come in a can
boys names that start with *R*
girls names that start with *M*

items that come in threes (for example, three blind mice)
items that are good luck (for example, a rabbit's foot)
girls names that are flowers
states that start with the letter *M*
articles of clothing that start with *S*
things you throw away

On the count of three, the challenge begins. How many items can you come up with in 2 minutes? At the end of the time limit, each player reads his list out loud. If an item listed is a bit of a stretch, be prepared to defend it. If the other players won't accept it, it does not count. It is all right for players to have the same items on a list. For example, two players might say Montana for the category States that begin with the letter *M*. The winner lists the most items.

For example, if the category is Items in a kitchen beginning with the letter *S*, you might list:

sink	spices	salad spinner	soap
saucepan	scissors	sponge	soup
spaghetti	soda	spoon	stove
spatula	strawberries	salt	sugar
salsa	stool	superglue	strainer

Twenty items with the letter S. Can you top that? Start a new round with another category.

Flashlight Tag

Number of players: 4 or more
Location: Outdoors at night
Equipment: A flashlight

Energy level: Action-packed
Type of game: Tagging

This is a classic nighttime tag game. Outline your playing field, such as the front yard. Agree on a home base, a place where players are safe and cannot be tagged. Select one player to be It and give her the flashlight.

On the count of three, all players run around. The object is for It to tag a player with the beam from the flashlight. There is only one rule concerning the flashlight: The light can be turned on only when It is about to tag a player. Once a player is illuminated, he is out and the flashlight is turned off until It tries to tag another player. Home base offers refuge at all times. When only one player is left, he is the winner and gets to be the new It.

If you can find a flashlight for each player, try this version, similar to the first but with a twist. If It tags you with the beam of the flashlight, you can save yourself by tagging It back with your light before he turns off his light. If you are successful, you are not out.

You can also play by hiding, one player to a hiding spot. The object is to seek out hidden players and tag them with the flashlight beam. The last player found is the winner and becomes the next It.

Look out for the light.

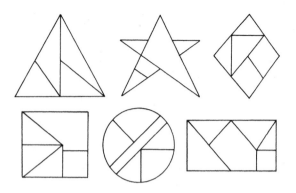

Shape Me

Number of players: 1 or more
Location: Indoors
Equipment: Scissors, a ruler, a pencil, and at least
  4 different colors of paper (preferably construction)
Energy level: Calm
Type of game: Arts/Imagination

Shapes, shapes, shapes! Lots of colors, lots of puzzles. Unravel the mystery of the different shapes. Play by yourself, with a friend, or with a group.

The object of this activity is to make basic shapes such as circles, rectangles, squares, and triangles, cut them into 4 to 6 pieces, mix up the pieces, and then reassemble the shapes. Eash shape is cut out of different colored paper. For example, to start with a circle, look for a round object to trace such as a cereal bowl, something at least 4 inches wide. Trace it onto a piece of colored paper. Creatively divide the circle, using the pencil and ruler, into at least 6 pieces. It's a greater challenge if the pieces are equal in size. Cut out the pieces of the shape.

If you are making a rectangle, make it large, at least 7 inches wide and 3½ inches tall. Divide it into at least 6 pieces. Make a square at least 5 inches on each side and cut it into a minimum of 5 pieces. For a triangle, make the base at least 6 inches and the sides 5 inches, and cut it into 4 or more pieces.

Decide on how many shapes to puzzle-ize. Outline, divide, and cut out each one. Shuffle the pieces of each shape. Take one shape. Can you reassemble it? Try each different shape. If you are playing with a group, have each player try one and then trade.

If you have mastered these puzzles, try some new shapes, such as a star, a diamond, a hexagon, or a pentagon. You decide on the size and number of pieces. Shape away!!

Two Truths and a Lie

Number of players: 3 or more
Location: Indoors or Outdoors
Equipment: None

Energy level: Calm
Type of game: Strategy

This is a fun way to get to know more about your friends and family.

Get comfortable. Sitting at a kitchen table, in the living room, or in a circle outside works best. Select a player to go first. She tells her friends 3 things about herself, 2 truths and 1 lie. The object is to make the lie totally believable. Can her friends figure out which one is the lie?

For example, Julia might say, "I like ice cream, my grandmother lives in Connecticut, and I have my own CD player." Which one is the lie? Believe it or not, Julia does not like ice cream. Lise might say, "My favorite color is purple, my cat's name is Story, and my favorite breakfast is waffles." Guess what! Story is not Lise's cat's name.

Play on, take turns, and see what you learn about your friends!

Steal the Bacon

Number of teams: 2 teams of at least 3 and 1 additional player to be the caller

Location: Outdoors

Equipment: A T-shirt, Frisbee, or ball

Energy level: Action-packed

Type of game: Racing

Bacon, bacon, who will steal the bacon? This is a classic racing game. Choose one player to be the caller. Divide the remaining players into 2 even teams. Choose an object that can be picked up easily to be the bacon, such as a T-shirt, Frisbee, or ball.

To begin, settle on the playing area, like the backyard. Divide the playing area in half, with each team taking a half. Within the half, select a base, at least 20 feet back, which is a safe zone. Put the bacon in the center of the field of play. The caller numbers the players on each team; for example, if you have 3 players on each team, each team has a player 1, a player 2, and a player 3. All players gather in their safe zone.

The object of this game is for the caller, who is standing in the center on one side, to shout out a number, say 2, and have both number-2 players race to steal the bacon. The player who captures the bacon must return to her base without being tagged by the caller. If she does, her team gets a point. If she is tagged, the other player walks the bacon back to the center and gets the point. The first team to reach 10 points wins. The next round begins with the bacon in the center again.

FUN FOR ALL AGES

Kick the Can

Number of players: 4 or more
Location: Outdoors
Equipment: An empty coffee can

Energy level: Action-packed
Type of game: Tagging

This is a time-honored classic most likely played by your parents and even your grandparents when they were your age. All you need is an empty coffee can, a group of friends, and the great outdoors.

Place the can in the middle of the playing area, choose a person to be It, and set the boundaries (for example, the backyard). All players gather in a circle around the can while the player who is It stands next to the can with closed eyes. It counts to 50 while the other players scatter and hide. On 50, he opens his eyes and goes looking for the other players while also trying to guard the can.

The object is for players to manage to come back from their hiding places and kick the can without being tagged by It. If someone is tagged, she is out and must watch the game from the sidelines. If she successfully gets back and kicks the can, she is safe. Be sure to put the can back in its starting place. Play continues until all players have been tagged or have kicked the can. The last person tagged is the next player to be It and places the can in the starting place while the other players assemble at the middle to start a new round.

Wink

Number of players: 5 or more
Location: Indoors
Equipment: A deck of cards

Energy level: Calm
Type of game: Guessing

Winking, blinking, guess who I am. Best with at least 5 players, and the more, the merrier. The object of the game is to have one player secretly wink (or blink if you do not know how to wink) all players out of existence, one at a time, until someone discovers who the winker is.

To choose the winker, use a deck of cards. All players agree on a suit, such as diamonds, and separate it from the deck. Shuffle the suit and deal the cards. Some players may be dealt more than one card. The player who receives the jack is the winker.

The game begins with everyone sitting around a table talking to one another while the winker looks around and secretly winks at those players who make eye contact with him. If you are winked at, you are out of the game, but you can enjoy hamming up your demise. Once everyone knows you are winked out, you can continue in the conversation and have fun watching everyone else drop. If a player has a guess who the winker is, she can say it, and if she's correct she chooses the next winker. If no one guesses correctly before all players get winked out, the winker decides who is next. To name the next winker, the chooser walks around the table and whispers in each player's ear whether or not it is that player by saying "yes" or "no." During this time, players can sing, hum, laugh, or make any noise to distract attention from the whispering.

Limbo

Number of players: 5 or more
Location: Outdoors
Equipment: A long straight stick like a mop
    or broom handle or a long rope

Energy level: Lively
Type of game: Balancing

Wanna limbo? How flexible are you?

    The object of this classic game is to walk under the stick or rope with your chin facing the sky at all times. Keep your back arched and your knees slightly bent. The stick starts high (the height of the tallest person playing) and, once everyone has passed under it, is lowered for the next round.

    Two players hold the ends of the stick while the rest try to go under. Take turns. In a large group, all players try to go under, one by one, at each height. For each new round, the stick is lowered.

Players are out if they touch or bump the stick in any way or if they crouch under the stick or bend at the waist. No crawling, walking on knees, or turning the head to the side or forward.

How low can you go?

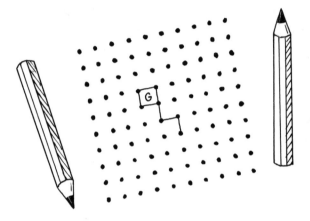

Dozens of Dots

Number of players: 2 to 3
Location: Indoors or Outdoors
Equipment: Pencils for each player and paper
Energy level: Calm
Type of game: Strategy

Dots, dots in a square—can you connect them and claim them as yours?

The object is to claim the most boxes by drawing the lines that close them and marking them with the initial of your first name. The winner has his initial in the most boxes when all dots are connected.

One player draws rows of dots, equally spaced horizontally and vertically. There must be the same number of dots across as down, making a perfect square. To start, draw 10 rows of 10 dots.

The youngest player begins the game, followed in turn by the player closest in age. On each turn, players draw a line connecting only 2 dots either horizontally or vertically; connecting diagonally is not allowed. On your turn, if your connection closes a box, you get to put your initial in the box and go again.

Strategic thinking is the key. As the game progresses, be sure to think through the connecting opportunities and consequences. Remember, any box that has three sides needs only one more line to complete it. Be careful not to allow your opponent the advantage of closing too many boxes. You'll often find that after the grid is marked with many incomplete boxes, one completing line will have a domino effect of allowing a player to complete many boxes in one turn.

Red Rover, Red Rover

Number of teams: 2 teams of at least 5
Location: Outdoors
Equipment: None

Energy level: Action-packed
Type of game: Running

Red Rover, Red Rover, let Austin come over. This is a great game for a large outdoor gathering. The object of this game is to run and break through the opposing team's line.

Play begins by dividing all players into 2 teams. Choose one team to go first. That team picks a leader whose job is to call to a player from the other side to come over.

The teams line up a fair distance apart, say about 20 feet, facing each other on the playing field. The members of each team stand shoulder to shoulder firmly holding hands to create a human fence. The links should be strong so they can survive someone trying to break through.

The leader selects a player from the other team—let's say Tony—and says, "Red Rover, Red Rover, let Tony come over." Tony runs toward the other team's line and tries to break through the human link by making two players let go of each other's hands. There's no slipping under arms or hurdling over them. If Tony cannot break through, he becomes part of that team. If Tony is successful, he chooses a player to accompany him back to his team. The game is over when one team has all the players.

Lots of laughs, lots of strategy, and great for all ages.

Rocket Blaster

Number of teams: 2 teams of at least 3
Location: Outdoors
Equipment: 2 markers and 2 batons

Energy level: Action-packed
Type of game: Relay

Blast off like a rocket in this classic relay game.

To start, settle on a playing area. Designate a start line and place a turnaround marker for each team. These markers can be T-shirts, baseball caps, or shoes, anything players can run around. Each team needs a baton, the rocket, to pass off after each lap; it can be a Frisbee, a stick, a ruler, etc.

Designate one player to say, "On your mark, get set, go," starting the race. The first player on each team, rocket in hand, races to the marker, runs around it, and runs back to the start line to hand off the rocket to the next player. This runner repeats the path and passes the rocket to the next in line. The objective of the game is to be the first team to finish the relay.

A second version uses a ball as the baton or rocket. The ball is held in place under one arm. If the ball drops, the player must start over.

Mysterious Mugs

Number of players or teams: 2 or more (if more, play in teams)
Location: Indoors or Outdoors
Energy level: Calm

Equipment: 3 identical mugs, cups, or shells and 1 small soft object
Type of game: Guessing

Can you guess which upside-down mug is hiding the treasure? This classic shell game hides objects under mugs, cups, or shells and tests your ability to find them.

Play with a partner or in teams. Find 3 identical mugs, cups (paper is fine), or shells and 1 small soft object to hide, such as a marshmallow, a piece of cereal, or a rubber ball (something that does not make a lot of noise when shuffled on a tabletop).

If you are playing with one other person, have your partner turn the three mugs upside down and place the marshmallow under one of them. As your partner watches, shuffle the mugs around, constantly rearranging their order, talking or singing the whole time to distract your partner. After thoroughly confusing your partner, line up the three mugs in a row. Can your partner guess which mug conceals the marshmallow? If her guess is correct, it is her turn to move the mugs; if not, you do it again.

For a group, divide into 2 teams and play for points. Each correct guess on a turn earns 1 point. The action remains the same. The first team to reach 10 points wins.

Frisky Fists and Flapping Feet

Number of players: 2 to 5

Location: Indoors or Outdoors on the grass

Equipment: None

Energy level: Lively

Type of game: Balancing

Remember that old favorite, stacking hands on top of one another? Well, this game uses fists and feet and could get a little frisky. The object of the game is for all players to stack their feet and fists on top of one another without collapsing. All players sit on the floor or the grass and take their shoes off. Sit across from each other if there are 2 players, in a circle if there are more. While keeping his knees bent, player 1 puts one foot in the middle of the circle. The next player puts a foot on top of player 1's foot. When every player has a foot on top of another foot, then player 1 adds his other foot and all players do the same in turn. Got the feet stacked? Now proceed in the same manner with each player's fists.

The silliness begins when the foot on the bottom of the foot pile moves to the top followed by the fist on the bottom of the fist pile moving to the top. Players alternate pulling a foot and a fist from the bottom and adding it to the top until the stacking collapses or they fall over laughing.

Windbag

Number of players or teams: 2 or more
   (if more, play in teams)
Location: Indoors or Outdoors

Equipment: A facial tissue for each player
Energy level: Lively
Type of game: Racing

Huff and puff and blow the tissue down the line. The objective is to blow the tissue from the beginning line to the end line and back again to the start. If you have 2 or 3 players, compete as individuals. If you have more players, divide into 2 teams. Play indoors or out with one tissue per player or team.

Settle on start and finish lines about 8 feet apart. If you're playing in teams, line each team up at the start line. The first player in each team line gets down on her knees and places the tissue on the start line. On the count of three, start. The object of this game is to blow the tissue to the end line and back while crawling. The first individual player to blow her tissue both ways wins. In teams, the next teammate on line repeats the tissue blow, and the first team to finish wins.

For a blustery and adventurous team challenge, stand each team in a line shoulder to shoulder. The object of this version is to blow the tissue from person to person. To do this, the first player on each team puts the tissue on his face. At the count of three, start. The "windbag" blasts the tissue into the air. The next player in line tries to catch it on the back of her hand. She puts it on her face without using her other hand and blows it to the next player's hand. Play continues until the last player catches it with his hand. The team to pass the tissue down the line first wins. If the tissue is dropped at any point, the team must start over with the first player.

Balloons Big Time

Number of players: 1 to 2
Location: Indoors or Outdoors
Energy level: Lively

Equipment: A few blown-up balloons, 10–12 inches
Type of game: Bouncing/Volley

This is a game of bouncy balloon activities. The object of this game is to perform tricks with balloons. Blow them up, knot them, and begin.

Try these tricks by yourself:

- Balance a balloon on your nose. Can you walk sideways? How long does it stay on?
- Juggle it on your thighs. How many can you do?
- Bounce it like a ball. Can you dribble it?
- Punch it in the air. How long can you keep it up before it falls?
- Bob it with your elbows. Can you pass it back and forth from elbow to elbow?

Try these tricks with a friend:

- Volley it back and forth with your hands. Can you volley using any part of your body except your hands, say your forehead, nose, feet, back, or hips?
- Bat it back and forth taking one step back each time. How far apart did you get?
- Standing back to back, about 4 feet apart, with your friend, kick it back and forth with your heels. How long can you keep it going?
- Create static electricity by rubbing the balloon against your stomach. What can you stick it to: Your friend, a wall, a door, a couch?

Hot days call for water balloons. Fill the balloons half full at the outside hose faucet and tie them. Now toss, pass, and throw one with your partner. How long before it bursts?

Spiderweb

Number of players: 3 or more

Location: Outdoors

Equipment: For each player: a ball of string,
2 sticks, and a different colored marker

Energy level: Lively

Type of game: Hunting

Spinning up and spinning down, spinning all around. Calling all spiders. Find several friends to join you and learn how to spin a web.

To start, go outside.

Step 1: Each player colors one end of her ball of string to identify it as hers.

Step 2: Tie the colored end of the string to your first stick and wrap the string round and round the stick until there is only 1 foot of string remaining. Color the last inch of the string.

Step 3: Now tie that loose end to your second stick and rest it on an agreed-upon starting point, such as a bush.

Step 4: When all the players have finished this phase, the oldest player in the group says, "On your mark, get set, spin," and all players begin to weave the web.

The object is for players to weave their strings off their sticks around bushes and trees, under swings, behind outdoor furniture, and so on, crisscrossing other players' strings, creating a giant web.

Step 5: When all the string is unwrapped from the sticks, players drop their sticks to the ground and return to the starting place.

Step 6: It is time to detangle. Players choose a string other than the one they created, which they can identify by their color marking. As you follow the string, wrap it around the stick until you reach the end.

You may bump into a fellow spider as you go through the web detangling the string wherever it leads you. There are no winners, no losers, just spiderwebs.

Silly Spoons

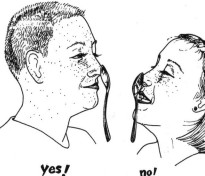

yes!   **no!**

Number of players: 1 or more
Location: Indoors or
   Outdoors
Energy level: Lively

Equipment: A teaspoon
   for each player
Type of game: Balancing

Slippery, saggy, silly spoons! Can you balance one on your nose? Go to the kitchen drawer and find a teaspoon.

Like juggling, this takes some practice. The thrill is in the accomplishment. Hold your head straight, face forward, and put the round part of the spoon on your nose with the handle pointing down. Tilting your head is allowed, but not resting the handle of the spoon on your chin. If the spoon keeps sliding off, try patting the bridge of your nose with a tissue. Can you find the way to balance?

With repetition, you'll be a spoon specialist. How long can you balance? Can you walk with the spoon balanced on your nose?

For a change, try balancing the back of the spoon across the bridge of your nose. Try dancing with it or jumping up and down. What other silly activities can you invent?

Sardines

Number of players: 4 or more
Location: Indoors or Outdoors
Equipment: None

Energy level: Lively
Type of game: Hiding and Seeking

Sneaky, slippery sardines. Can you find them? This classic hide-and-seek game works in any setting as long as you have 4 sardines . . . Everyone has to agree on the specific area that can be used for hiding, such as only the upstairs, the basement, or the backyard.

To begin, choose one person, the sardine, to hide alone while everyone else closes their eyes and counts to 100. All players go off in search of the hidden sardine. Once someone finds the hidden player, he joins her in hiding, but continues to be quiet so that other players don't follow the giggles to the secret hiding place.

Whoever is the last to find this group ends the game and gets to be the sneaky, slippery sardine for the next round.

Tug-of-War

Number of teams: 2 teams of at least 5
Location: Outdoors
Energy level: Action-packed
Type of game: Tugging

Equipment: A long rope at least 25 feet long, a piece of ribbon or string, and 3 sticks or tape

A classic for any large neighborhood, family, or beach gathering. A rope at least 25 feet long, muscle power, and stamina are the necessary ingredients.

Divide into 2 teams and lay the rope down on the playing field. Find the center of the rope and mark it with a ribbon or string. On the ground beneath the center of the rope, mark the center dividing line with a stick or tape. Now measure 3 feet from the center ground line on both sides and mark the spots with the other sticks or tape. These lines mark the starting lines behind which each team lines up at the beginning of the game.

Each team falls in line along the rope facing the opposing team. Each player grips the rope tightly with both hands. It's best to position the strongest and tallest players of each team at the ends of the rope.

The object is to pull the opposing team toward you so that the center ribbon on the rope crosses your start line. Who has the might? Who has the muscle? Try again, mixing up the teams.

Ha, Ha, Ha

Number of players: 4 or more
Location: Indoors or Outdoors
Equipment: None

Energy level: Lively
Type of game: Laughing

This game is a bellyful of laughs. The object is to pass the word *Ha* down the line without laughing. The first player lies down on his back on the ground. Player 2 lies down with her head, face up, on player 1's stomach. Player 3 lies down with his head, face up, on player 2's stomach. Repeat this arrangement for as many players as are in the group.

Player 1 starts the game by saying, "Ha." In turn, each player adds a *Ha*. Player 2 says, "Ha, Ha," and player 3 says, "Ha, Ha, Ha," and so on down the line. Can you do it without laughing? How far down the line do you get? Reorder the line occasionally.

You can also play trying to pass silent belly giggles—laughter without noise or words—down the line. You'll find that laughing is contagious.

Spud

Number of players: 5 or more
Location: Outdoors
Equipment: A soft/medium-size ball

Energy level: Action-packed
Type of game: Throwing/Catching

This age-old group game involves running, throwing, and catching.

Gather everyone together in a circle and number all players, starting at 1 and counting until everyone has a number. Choose one person to be the first to throw the ball.

At the count of three, that player throws the ball up in the air and calls out a number while the other players run and scatter. The player whose number was called runs to catch and pick up the ball. When he does, he yells, "Freeze," and all players must instantly stand still. He is allowed to take 3 steps in any direction.

The object of this game is to tag a frozen player below the waist with the ball. Frozen players can do anything to avoid the ball as long as one foot stays in place. If the ball hits a player, she takes the letter S in SPUD. If the ball misses a player, he takes the letter S. As the rounds continue, any player who accumulates all the letters—S-P-U-D—is out.

For the next round, the player who earned the S throws the ball up in the air and calls out a number. In each round, whoever earns a letter is the next player to throw the ball. Play continues until there is only one player left.

Penny Pitch

Number of players: 2 or more
Location: Indoors or Outdoors
Equipment: 3 pennies,
   6 cups, and a bandanna

Energy level: Lively
Type of game: Tossing

Powerfully pitching for points—the object of this game is to pitch pennies into cups arranged in a triangle for points.

Line up the cups in this order:
Row 1 has 1 cup.
Row 2, 3 inches below row 1, has 2 cups each about 3 inches apart.
Row 3, 3 inches below row 2, has 3 cups each about 3 inches apart.

Each row is worth a different number of points. The top cup is worth 50 points, the cups in row 2 are each worth 20 points, and the cups in row 3 are each worth 10 points.

Once the cups have been arranged, take 20 giant steps backward from the third row of cups and mark the pitching line. A player cannot step over this line. Each player, in turn, pitches 3 pennies. Play in rounds. The first player to reach 100 points wins.

Now try this blindfolded. Use a bandanna to cover your eyes and take turns pitching blindfolded. How did you all do this time? Did it take longer to get to 100?

Dodgeball

Number of teams: 2 teams of at least 3
Location: Outdoors
Equipment: 2 soft medium-size balls, and a center field marker

Energy level: Action-packed
Type of game: Dodging

To set up the field for this age-old classic game, use your center field marker, which can be anything from a jump rope to an old T-shirt or a line drawn with chalk, to divide the playing field in half.

Separate the players into 2 teams. The object of this game is to dodge the ball thrown by the opposing team. Two balls will be tossed at once, one from each side, so beware.

A few rules: Teams cannot cross the centerline or step out of the playing field's boundaries. Tagging with the ball must be below the waist; tagging above is a no-no—if you do it, you are out of the game. If you are hit by the ball, you switch to the other team. If you catch the ball in midair, the person who threw it joins your team. If you drop it immediately after catching it, you join the other team. The game ends when there are no players left on one side.

Another version of this game is to choose one player to stand in the middle and dodge balls thrown from the back line of the playing field. It is fast; it still uses 2 balls but they're not tossed at the same time. To begin, a player from one team throws the ball at the "artful dodger" in the center. If the dodger is hit, he and the thrower exchange places. If not, the ball is now thrown by the other team. Again, tagging above the waist is an automatic out.

Straw Power

Number of players: 2 or more
Location: Indoors or Outdoors
Energy level: Lively

Type of game: Racing
Equipment: Drinking straws
and 10 lightweight food objects

The object of this game is to be the first to transfer 10 food objects from point A to point B using a straw. The winner is the player who completes the race first with the most intact food.

For each player you need a drinking straw and 10 lightweight food objects such as dry cereal, popcorn, potato chips, or other food items larger than the straw's opening. Decide on the foods. Choose the beginning and end lines, about 6 feet apart. Be sure the path is clear for all players in the race. Create a pile of 10 items for each player. Pick up your straw and practice inhaling as if you were drinking. Got the motion? This action attaches a piece of food to the end of the straw. It's best to attach the straw to the middle of the piece of food.

On the count of three, all players begin transferring one piece of food at a time from the start to the end line. When one piece is deposited at the end line, go back and race with another piece. Repeat until all the food is at the end line. If you drop your item along the path, pick it up, return to the beginning line, and start all over with it. Remember, the player with the most intact food wins.

Do you have the lung power? Go ahead and lengthen the path. Try other foods. Try mixing foods. What works? What doesn't? Your pet, if you have one, can clean up by eating.

Candle Tag

Number of teams: 2 teams of at least 4
Location: Outdoors
Energy level: Action-packed

Equipment: Day, none; night, a flashlight for each player
Type of game: Tagging

Help . . . I'm melting. Save me. Don't let the candle go out! This is team tag and everybody is a candle. The object of this game is to tag all the members of the other team so that they melt to the ground. Gather your group together and divide into two teams. Select one person on each team to be It—the one who has the power to melt candles.

On the count of three, everyone runs around while both Its try to tag someone on the opposite team. Once tagged, that player begins to melt, slowly shrinking to the ground. She can be saved if one of her teammates tags her back to life. If the candle melts completely, then she must sit on the ground until the game is over. Each It tries to tag all the candles from the opposite team so that there are no flames left. Next round, mix up your teams and try it again.

If you are playing at night, have your friends bring flashlights. Play the same way, but as you melt, hold the flashlight so the beam points toward the sky. If you melt all the way to the ground, turn off your flashlight.

Octopus Tag

Number of players: 4 or more
Location: Outdoors
Equipment: "Treasures" and a ball

Energy level: Action-packed
Type of game: Tagging

The octopus is using its many long arms to protect its treasures in this classic tag game. To play, you'll need to collect as many "treasures" as you have players. Treasures can be anything: a bean-bag toy, a plastic cup, swim goggles, a lunch box, whatever you can find. You also need a ball for the octopus. The object of this game is to steal the octopus's treasures and bring them back to base without being tagged.

The octopus places its treasures in a line, takes a step backward, and turns away holding the ball. Players try to sneak up behind the octopus and steal its treasures, carrying them back to a predetermined base, the safe zone, without being tagged.

All players start at the base. Each player decides when to make a move. As quietly as possible, make your way to the treasure to steal whatever you can. If the octopus hears you or thinks you are near, it will turn around and try to catch you by tagging you below the waist with the ball. If you are tagged, go to the octopus den, the area behind the treasures. The only way out is if one of your mates runs into the den and tags and releases you before you are both caught and tagged with the ball by the octopus. If all the treasures are successfully seized, the game starts over with a new octopus.

Blindman's Buff

Number of players: 6 or more
Location: Outdoors
Equipment: A bandanna or a scarf
Energy level: Action-packed
Type of game: Blindfold/Guessing

Can you guess the identity of a player while blindfolded?
Try it and see in this classic game.

Collect in a circle and choose someone to be It, the
blindman, who stands in the center of the circle blind-
folded. It counts to 15 while everyone in the circle moves clockwise around her. On 15, she shouts,
"Freeze." At this, all players stop; then each player takes 2 steps in any direction. The blindman
then wanders around inside the circle with her arms extended until she touches someone.

The object of this game is to confuse the blindman so that when she touches you, she doesn't
know who you are. The blindman is allowed only one touch. If she correctly guesses who you are,
you are the next blindman. If she is incorrect, the other players tell her so and she has to find
another player to identify. She has only 2 chances to identify players. If she can't correctly identify
someone, the group selects the next It.

Here are some ways to disguise yourself from It: Use a fake voice. Stoop down or bend your
knees when you freeze so It won't recognize your height. To seem taller, stand on your tiptoes.

Obstacle Course

Number of players: 2 or more
Location: Outdoors
Equipment: Obstacle objects

Energy level: Action-packed
Type of game: Obstacle

Limber up and get ready to move! The challenges of this game are the creativity in designing the course and the agility in moving through it in the least amount of time. Two or more players can enjoy this outside game.

Use your imagination; anything goes—hoses, bushes, hula hoops, boxes, trees, steps, sports equipment, or lawn furniture. All can be used as obstacles to jump over, crawl under, go around, or run through. The more twists and turns and highs and lows in the course, the better.

Set up the course. A course might include jumping 3 times in a hula hoop lying on the ground, then jumping over a box, running 2 times around a tree, leaping over a bush, hopping up steps, skipping over a baseball bat, jumping over a bike helmet, sitting in a lawn chair, and finishing by crawling over a hose.

One player goes through the course at a time. Take turns. Once the players are familiar with how to move, have someone time each player. If you do not have a watch, have the timer count off seconds (one thousand one, one thousand two, etc). The object is to beat your personal best. If everyone can master the course, make it harder or try doing it backward.

INDEX
Games

Type of Game

Activity Level of Game

CALM